First World War
and Army of Occupation
War Diary
France, Belgium and Germany

61 DIVISION
Divisional Troops
305 Brigade Royal Field Artillery
1 May 1915 - 17 September 1916

WO95/3042/2

The Naval & Military Press Ltd
www.nmarchive.com
Published in association with The National Archives

Published by

The Naval & Military Press Ltd

Unit 10 Ridgewood Industrial Park,

Uckfield, East Sussex,

TN22 5QE England

Tel: +44 (0) 1825 749494

www.naval-military-press.com

www.nmarchive.com

This diary has been reprinted in facsimile from the original. Any imperfections are inevitably reproduced and the quality may fall short of modern type and cartographic standards.

© **Crown Copyright**
Images reproduced by permission of The National Archives, London, England, 2015.

Contents

Document type	Place/Title	Date From	Date To
Heading	WO95/3042/2		
Heading	61 Division 305 Bde R.F.A. Formerly 2/1 South Midland Gloucester Bde Rfa 1915 May-1916 Mar		
Heading	2nd/1 2/1 South Midland Bde R.F.A. May 1915 To Match 1916		
Miscellaneous			
Miscellaneous	Agreement		
Miscellaneous	Scheme For Boarding Out Army Horses & Mules		
Miscellaneous	War Diaries	04/05/1916	04/05/1916
War Diary	Writtle	01/05/1915	21/05/1915
Miscellaneous	War Diary	04/06/1915	04/06/1915
War Diary	Writtle	01/06/1915	30/06/1915
Miscellaneous	2/1st South Midland.	02/07/1915	02/07/1915
War Diary	Writtle	01/07/1915	04/07/1915
War Diary	Chelmsford	05/07/1915	05/07/1915
War Diary	Mill Green	05/07/1915	06/07/1915
War Diary	Erittle	06/07/1915	22/07/1915
War Diary	Chelmsford	23/07/1915	24/07/1915
War Diary	Epping	26/07/1915	30/07/1915
War Diary	2/1st South Midland.	05/07/1915	05/07/1915
War Diary	Epping	01/08/1915	05/08/1915
War Diary	Gt Baddow	06/07/1915	07/07/1915
War Diary	Epping	08/08/1915	18/08/1915
War Diary	Lexden	18/08/1915	18/08/1915
War Diary	Great Bently	19/08/1915	19/08/1915
War Diary	Epping	19/08/1915	26/08/1915
War Diary	Gt. Baddow	28/08/1915	29/08/1915
War Diary	Epping	29/08/1915	31/08/1915
Miscellaneous	2/1st South Midland	03/09/1915	03/09/1915
Miscellaneous	2/1st South Midland.	03/09/1915	03/09/1915
War Diary	Epping	02/09/1915	04/09/1915
War Diary	Ingatestone	05/09/1915	30/09/1915
War Diary	Epping	02/09/1915	04/09/1915
War Diary	Ingatestone	05/09/1915	30/09/1915
Miscellaneous	61st South Midland	05/10/1915	05/10/1915
War Diary	Ingatestone	01/10/1915	30/10/1915
War Diary	Ingatestone	01/10/1915	01/10/1915
Miscellaneous	61st South Midland	03/11/1915	03/11/1915
Miscellaneous	War Diary-Or-Intelligence Summary.	19/10/1915	19/10/1915
Miscellaneous	2/1st South Midland Brigade R.F.A.	29/10/1916	29/10/1916
War Diary	Ingatestone	01/11/1915	30/11/1915
Miscellaneous	61st South Midland	03/12/1915	03/12/1915
Miscellaneous	2/1st South Midland Brigade	04/11/1915	04/11/1915
Miscellaneous	2/1st South Midland Brigade R.F.A.	04/11/1915	04/11/1915
Miscellaneous	Appendix No.2. 2/1st South Midland (Gloucestershire) Brigade. R.F.A.	05/11/1915	05/11/1915
Heading	War Diary of 2/1st South Midland Glos Brigade, R.F.A. From 1st December, 1915 To 31st December, 1915 Volume1.		

Heading	War Diary of 2/1st South Midland Glos Brigade, R.F.A. From 1st December, 1915 To 31st December, 1915 Volume 1.		
War Diary	Ingatestone	01/12/1915	28/12/1915
Miscellaneous	Appendix ' A ' Allotment to Batteries of 18 pr Guns And Wagons		
Heading	War Diary of 2/1st South Midland Glos Brigade, R.F.A. From 1st January, 1916 To 31st January, 1916 To 31st January 1916		
War Diary	Ingatestone Essex	01/01/1916	31/01/1916
Miscellaneous	2/1st South Midland Brigade R.F.A.	14/01/1916	14/01/1916
Miscellaneous	2/1st South Midland Brigade R.F.A.	27/01/1916	27/01/1916
Heading	War Diary of 2/1st South Midland Glos Brigade, R.F.A. from 1st January, 1916 To 31st January, 1916 Volume 2.		
War Diary	Ingatestone Essex	01/01/1916	31/01/1916
Miscellaneous	2/1st South Midland Brigade R.F.A.	14/01/1916	14/01/1916
Miscellaneous	2/1st South Midland Brigade R.F.A.	27/01/1916	27/01/1916
Heading	War Diary of 2/1st South Midland Glos Brigade, R.F.A. From 1st February,1916 To 29th February, 1916		
War Diary	Ingatestone Essex	01/02/1916	27/02/1916
War Diary	Bulford	29/02/1916	29/02/1916
Miscellaneous	Daily Orders Part II	05/02/1916	05/02/1916
Miscellaneous	Daily Orders. Part II	12/02/1915	12/02/1915
Miscellaneous	Daily Orders. Part II	12/05/1916	12/05/1916
Miscellaneous	Daily Orders. Part II	12/02/1916	12/02/1916
Miscellaneous	Daily Orders. Part II	19/02/1916	19/02/1916
Miscellaneous	Daily Orders Part II	26/02/1916	26/02/1916
Miscellaneous	For Information Of The A.G.'s Office At The Base.	26/02/1916	26/02/1916
Heading	War Diary of 2/1st South Midland (Glos) Brigade, R.F.A. From 1st March,1916 To 31st March, 1916 Volume No. 4.		
War Diary	No.7 Camp Bulford	01/03/1916	02/03/1916
War Diary	Larkhill	03/03/1916	08/03/1916
War Diary	Bulford	08/03/1916	08/03/1916
War Diary	Larkhill	05/03/1916	05/03/1916
War Diary	Bulford	05/03/1916	06/03/1916
War Diary	Larkhill	07/03/1916	07/03/1916
War Diary	Bulford	08/03/1916	10/03/1916
War Diary	No. 7 Camp, Bulford	11/03/1916	31/03/1916
Heading	61st Division 305th Brigade R.F.A. 1916 May-1916 Sep		
Heading	305 Bde RFA May 1915		
Heading	HQ G.S. of Div Vol XXI		
Heading	War Diary of 305th Brigade RFA Late 2/1 SM Bde from 22nd May 1916 to 31st May 1916		
War Diary	Amesbury Salisbury Plain	22/05/1916	22/05/1916
War Diary	Harve France	23/05/1916	25/05/1916
War Diary	Haverskerque	28/05/1916	31/05/1916
Miscellaneous	Appendix No. 1		
Miscellaneous	Brigade State Appendix No 2	22/05/1916	22/05/1916
Diagram etc	Appendix 3		
Miscellaneous	Order of Battle 61st (South Midland) Division Appendix 4		
Map			

Heading	War Diary of 305th Brigade RFA From 1st June 1916 to 30th June 1916 (Volume No. 2 Overseas)		
War Diary	Haverskerque	01/06/1916	30/06/1916
Heading	War Diary of 305th Brigade RFA Volume 3 July 1st-July 31st 1916		
Heading	War Diary of 305th Brigade RFA From 1st July 1916 to 31st July 1916 (Volume No. 3 Overseas)		
War Diary		01/07/1916	31/07/1916
Heading	War Diary of 305th Brigade RFA Aug 1st to 31st 1916 Volume 4		
Heading	War Diary of 305th Brigade RFA From 1st August 1916 to 31st August 1916 (Volume No. 4 Overseas)		
War Diary	In the field	04/08/1916	31/08/1916
Heading	War Diary Late 305th Art Bde Sept 1st-17th 1916 Vol V		
Heading	War Diary 305th Brigade RFA From 1st September 1916 to 17th September 1916		
War Diary	Laventie	02/09/1916	02/09/1916
War Diary	Nouveau Monde	02/09/1916	17/09/1916

WO 95/3042/2

61 DIVISION

305 BDE RFA

formerly 2/1 SOUTH MIDLAND GLOUCESTER BDE
RFA

1915 MAY. — 1916 MAR

Locks 21.5.15 - 31.5.15

2nd/1.

2/1 South Midland Bde.
R.F.A.

May 1915 to March 1916

355 BDE

61 DIV

2115.

(b) Upon Mobilisation the Borrower shall deliver the horse, within twenty-four hours of notification by the Military Authorities, to any place named by them, provided that it is not more than ten miles distant from the stables of the Borrower, and upon receipt of the horse the Agreement shall be considered as terminated, and no compensation or refund of any unexpired portion of the annual payment will be made by the Military Authorities.

12. The Borrower shall pay annually in advance to such person as the Military Authorities may appoint a sum of £7 10s. 0d. for the use of each horse. All veterinary expenses and medicine will be provided free of charge by the Military Authorities.

13. If the Borrower commits a breach of any of the provisions of this Agreement, or dies, or becomes bankrupt, or a Receiving Order or Order for Administration be made against him or in respect of his estate, or any execution or distress be levied on his goods, or if he enters into, makes or executes any deed of arrangement as defined by the Deeds of Arrangement Act, 1914, or other composition or arrangement with or assignment for the benefit of his creditors, or purports to do so; or, in the case of a Company, an effective resolution is passed or an order is made for winding up, whether voluntary or otherwise; or if in the opinion of the Military Authorities it is undesirable that the horse should continue to remain in his possession, the Military Authorities have the right forthwith to terminate the Agreement and resume possession of the horse without notice or payment of compensation, or the return of any unexpired portion of the annual payment.

14. Subject to determination as provided in the foregoing clauses the Borrower shall keep the horse, or any horse which may be substituted therefor, for the period of one year from the date when the first horse was received by the Borrower, and at the expiration of that period shall continue to keep the horse, subject to three months' notice in writing of his intention to terminate this Agreement. In the event of such termination before the end of a complete year it shall rest with the Military Authorities (whose decision shall be final) to determine what proportion (if any) of the annual payment shall be refunded in respect of the unexpired period.

15. In the event of the Borrower keeping any one horse continuously (periods in Veterinary Hospital and of use by the Military Authorities under clause 11 (a) only excepted) for six consecutive years it shall thereupon become the property of the Borrower without any further payment, and this Agreement and everything herein contained shall be deemed to be determined. Notwithstanding anything herein contained and notwithstanding any termination of this Agreement under any of the foregoing provisions, the Borrower shall be responsible for the proper care of every horse until it has been returned to the Military Authorities.

16. In case of any dispute or disagreement as to the construction or meaning of any clause of this Agreement, or as to the due performance thereof, or as to any question arising thereunder, the decision of the Secretary of State, or of any person appointed by him to determine the matter, shall be final and conclusive.

SCHEDULE.

(Description of Horses subject to this Agreement.)

AGREEMENT.

An Agreement made the _____ day of _____ 191 .

between _____

on behalf of HIS MAJESTY'S PRINCIPAL SECRETARY OF STATE FOR THE WAR DEPARTMENT

(hereinafter called "the Secretary of State") of the one part, and _____

of _____

(hereinafter called "the Borrower") of the other part, whereby it is agreed as follows:—

    1. In this Agreement the term "Military Authorities" shall mean any officer for the time being duly appointed by the Secretary of State for the purpose of acting on his behalf in respect of this Agreement. The word "horse" shall include a mule, provided that a mule shall not be substituted for a horse or a horse for a mule under clause 7 or 8 without the consent of the Borrower. The word "month" means a calendar month.

    2. This Agreement relates to every horse specified in the Schedule hereto, or substituted therefor in pursuance of clause 7 or 8. Every such horse shall remain the property of the Secretary of State.

    3. Every horse will be delivered free of charge to the Borrower to the railway station specified by him, and not less than 7 days' notice of dispatch will be given by the Military Authorities. Free railway carriage will also be provided in respect of every horse returned in pursuance of this Agreement, unless it be returned on termination of the agreement pursuant to clauses 13 or 14 hereof, when the Borrower shall be responsible for the expense of returning it.

    4. Every horse before dispatch will be examined and passed by an Army Veterinary Officer as being free from symptoms of disease, but no liability will rest upon the Secretary of State in the event of any alleged error in such certificate, and no warranty is given. If the Borrower does not make any objection to the horse within two days of its delivery to him he shall be deemed to have agreed that it was sound and free from disease when delivered to him.

    5. While the horse is in the possession of the Borrower the Borrower shall—

    (a) At his own expense properly stable, care for, feed and keep it suitably shod;

    (b) Have the use of it for all reasonable work, but not for racing of any description or for carting unduly heavy loads, or purposes which the Military Authorities may deem likely to interfere with its usefulness for military requirements;

    (c) Not, without the consent of the Military Authorities, allow it to be hogged (unless already so) or docked, nor let it on hire or part with the possession of it, nor allow it to be "turned away" to grass.

    6. The Borrower shall at all times afford reasonable facilities to representatives of the Military Authorities for regular inspection of the horse and for checking mileage, hours and loads, and in particular, on receipt of at least four days' notice the Borrower shall, if required, once in every six months bring or cause to be brought the horse to a place of inspection, distant not more than 10 miles from the Borrower's stable, to be appointed by the Military Authorities.

    7. If the horse is injured, or becomes unsound or incapable of work or unfit for military purposes, or is or becomes unsuitable for the work for which the Borrower is entitled to use it—

    (a) The Borrower shall immediately notify the Veterinary Surgeon appointed by the Military Authorities;

    (b) The Borrower shall (if required) continue to keep the horse at his expense, but not for a longer period than one month, the Military Authorities providing Veterinary Attendance (including medicine) during the period;

    (c) The Borrower, if he has not been required to continue to keep it one month, shall return it at once to the Military Authorities, and if he has been required to continue to keep it one month shall, at the end of such month, if the horse is then still incapable of work or unfit for military purposes or unsuitable for the work for which the Borrower is entitled to use it, return it to the Military Authorities, and in either case the Military Authorities may within one month of its return replace it.

    8. If the horse dies while in the possession of the Borrower he shall give notice in writing to that effect to the Military Authorities, who may replace it within one month of the date of the notice.

    9. If the Military Authorities do not in accordance with clauses 7 or 8 replace any horse within the time therein mentioned to the reasonable satisfaction of the Borrower, the Agreement shall be regarded as terminated in respect of the horse not replaced, and it shall rest with the Military Authorities (whose decision shall be final) to determine what proportion (if any) of the annual payment shall be refunded in respect of the unexpired period.

    10. If the horse shall die, or be injured, or become unfit for military service, and such death, injury, or unfitness shall, in the opinion of the Military Authorities, have been caused by neglect or default on the part of the Borrower, the Borrower shall pay damages not exceeding £60, to be assessed by the Military Authorities.

    11. The Military Authorities shall, if so desired by them, have the exclusive use of the horse—

    (a) For any sixteen consecutive days in every year. The Military Authorities shall give the Borrower not less than fourteen days' notice of the date on which they will require such horse, and the Borrower shall, if desired, deliver the horse to the Military Authorities at any place appointed by them, provided that such place is not more than ten miles from the stables of the Borrower, the Military Authorities at the expiration of the term returning the horse either to the stables of the Borrower or to the appointed railway station;

Army Form W. 5095.

SCHEME FOR BOARDING OUT ARMY HORSES & MULES.

FORM OF APPLICATION.

To

HIS MAJESTY'S PRINCIPAL SECRETARY OF STATE FOR THE WAR DEPARTMENT.

I/We _____

Fill in description of business.

of _____

_____

hereby apply for the undermentioned animals, or so many of them as you may think fit, to be allotted to me/us upon the terms of an agreement in the form set out on the back of this Application.

I/We undertake to have suitable premises ready for the reception of any animal or animals which may be allotted to me/us in pursuance of this Application, and to execute an Agreement in the form set out on the back of this Application in respect of any animal which may be so allotted.

Animals applied for.

No.

*Strike out description of animals not required.

*Horses _____

*Mules _____

(Signature) _____

(Address) _____

Date _____

SUBJECT:- WAR DIARIES

From:-
    Officer Commanding,
    2/1st South Midland (Glos) Bde, RFA.

To:-
    Colonel-in-charge,
    Territorial Force Records
    Coten End, Warwick.

Sir,

    Herewith copies of War Diaries in respect of the Brigade under my Command for the following months:-

1915	1916
May	January
June	February
July	March
August	
September	
October	
November	
December	

Please keep these in your charge.

    I have the honour to be,
        Sir,
        Your obedient Servant,

                Lt.Colonel
                Commanding

No.7 Camp,
BULFORD
4th May, 1916

Army Form C. 2118.

WAR DIARY
or
INTELLIGENCE SUMMARY.
(Erase heading not required.)

Instructions regarding War Diaries and Intelligence Summaries are contained in F. S. Regs., Part II. and the Staff Manual respectively. Title pages will be prepared in manuscript.

F 375

Place	Date	Hour	Summary of Events and Information	Remarks and references to Appendices
Writtle.	May. 1.		25 Horses apportioned to Brigade.	
	2.		2/Lieut Cope & 2/Lieut Harris detailed for Map Reading Course.	
			2/Lieut Lascelles & Corporal Taylor for Musketry Course.	
			Combined Reconnaissance by Battery Staffs.	
		8.30	Night March.	
	4.	11a.m	Inspection of 1st Re-inforcements Kit.	
		5.p.m	Lecture by Commanding Officer on Gunnery.	
	5.	5.p.m	Lecture by Lieut Jenkins on Morse Code.	
	6.	5.p.m	Lecture by Adjutant. Military Law.	
	7.	5.15.	Lecture by Lt. Col Tunbridge. "Artillery & Aircraft".	
	8.		Lieut. Colonel Metford detailed for Instruction in Court Martial.	
	10.		Two N.C.O's detailed to attend Course in Cold Shoeing.	
		9.15 am	Driving Drill by Batteries commenced.	
	12.		Sketching Class for Officers under B.S.M. Bishop.	
			Screened Gun Epaulments and Trenches dug by 3rd Battery.	
	13.	2.15 pm	115 men Inoculated.	

1577 Wt.W10791/1773 500,000 1/15 D.D.&L. A.D.S.S./Forms/C. 2118.

Army Form C. 2118.

WAR DIARY
or
INTELLIGENCE SUMMARY.
(Erase heading not required.)

Instructions regarding War Diaries and Intelligence Summaries are contained in F. S. Regs., Part II. and the Staff Manual respectively. Title pages will be prepared in manuscript.

Place	Date	Hour	Summary of Events and Information	Remarks and references to Appendices
Writtle.	May 13.	11 am	Lecture by Adjutant on Court Martial Procedure. (Wet day).	
	14.		Inspection by C.R.A. of Battery Gun Drill in Epaulments.	
	14.		Lecture by Lieut Holmes on "Use & Care of Telephones"	
	15.		60 Horses apportioned to Brigade.	
			40 men Inoculated.	
	16.		Dummy Ammunition made for 90 M/M Guns.	
	17.	8.30.	Captain B.C. Biggar appointed Adjutant.	
	18.		Night March.	
	19.		Screened Gun Epaulments & Trenches dug by Ammunition Column.	
			Huts occupied by 240 men of 2nd & 3rd Batteries. 2nd & 3rd Battery Offices moved to Huts.	
			Lecture by Lieut Holmes on "Use & Care of Telephones"	
	20.	6.30.	Cross Country run for Brigade as physical exercise.	
		9.am	Course of Rifle Instruction started for all Recruits. Inspection by C.R.A.	
		5.30.	Tactical Scheme in Wylands Park.	
			Lecture by Major Berkely Hill on Military Law.	
	21.	12 Noon	Kit Inspection of 1st Re-inforcements.	

WAR DIARY.

Unit. 2/1st South Midland (Gloucestershire) Brigade R.F.A.

Division. 2/1st South Midland.

Mobolization Centre. Bristol.

Temporary War Station.

Stations since occupied subsequent to Concentration:-
                                            Northampton.
                                            Broomfield.
                                            Writtle.

(a). MOBOLIZATION. Nil.

(b). CONCENTRATION AT WAR STATIONS. (Including Railway Moves) Nil.

(c). ORGANIZATION FOR DEFENCE. (Including Vulnerable Points) Nil.

(d). TRAINING. Considerably handicapped owing to want of Modern Guns and Equipment: also with number of Horses with Pnuemonia and Ringworm segregated.

(e). DISCIPLINE. Improving steadily.

(f). ADMINISTRATION.

    1. Medical Services. Civilian Practitioner.

    2. Veterinary Services. Poor.

    3. Supply Services. Nil.

    4. Transport Services. Nil.

    5. Ordnance Services. Nil.

    6. Channels of Correspondence in Routine matters. Nil.

    7. Billeting and Hutting. Nil.

    8. Range Construction. Nil.

    9. Supply of Remounts. Improving. Stamp of horse satisfactory.

(g). RE-ORGANIZATION OF T. F. INTO HOME & IMPERIAL SERVICE. Nil.

(h). PREPARATION OF UNITS FOR IMPERIAL SERVICE. Percentage of Inoculated men steadily rising.

Station. Writtle, Essex.   Lieut. Colonel.
                                                      Commanding.

Date. June 4th 1915.

WAR DIARY
or
INTELLIGENCE SUMMARY.

(Erase heading not required.)

Army Form C. 2118.

Place	Date	Hour	Summary of Events and Information	Remarks and references to Appendices
WRITTLE.	1915. JUNE. 1st.		156 Sets New Harness issued to Batteries and Ammunition Column.	
	2nd		Lecture by Major Berkeley Hill on Military Law.	
	3rd		Inspection of Horses by Colonel Long C.B. Inspector General of Army Remounts.	
	7th		Inspection of Sick Horses by A.D.V.S. 3rd Army. Lecture by Lieut. Colonel Metford. V.D. on Driving. Course of Map Reading for N.C.O's commences.	
	8th		Course of Lectures on Gunnery every Monday Tuesday and Wednesday for Officers & N.C.O's by Mr. Whitehead commences. Night Digging. 1st Battery.	
	10.		Inspection by General Sir Leslie Rundle.	
	11.		26 men Inoculated.	
			Night Digging. 2nd Battery commenced.	
	12.		Major Austin proceeds on a Course of Instruction with the Expeditionary Force in France. Lecture by Staff Sergeant Cotton on Pay Duties. 120 Japanese Rifles issued out to Batteries and Ammunition Column. Private P.T. Rowe gazetted 2/Lieut to 2/1st S.M. Bde (Glos) R.F.A. Lieutenants Metford, Jenkins, and Harrison Gazetted Captains. 2/Lieut Harris Gazetted Lieut.	

Army Form C. 2118.

WAR DIARY
or
INTELLIGENCE SUMMARY.
(Erase heading not required.)

Instructions regarding War Diaries and Intelligence Summaries are contained in F. S. Regs., Part II. and the Staff Manual respectively. Title pages will be prepared in manuscript.

Place	Date 1915. JUNE.	Hour	Summary of Events and Information	Remarks and references to Appendices
WRITTLE.	14.		Night Digging. 3rd Battery commenced.	
	15.		Court of Enquiry held on No 1708 Driver Williams: having broken his leg.	
			2/Lieut. Lanham attached to Headquarters, Royal Artillery for Instruction.	
			Medical Board held on eleven men for Discharge.	
			Combined Battery Driving Drill re-commences.	
			No 2093. Sergeant Harris commences a 14 days Veterinary Course.	
			No 2053. Gunner Thomas sentenced to 168 hours detention for sleeping at his post.	
	16.		Night Digging Ammunition Column commenced.	
	18.		26 men Inoculated.	
	19.		Musketry Course commences. One Officer and two N.C.O's to attend.	
	20.		46 horses brought up from sick lines. (pneumonia)	
	22.		Series of Section Inspections by Commanding Officer commences.	
	24.		10 horses received from Remount Depot.	
	25.		Captain C.K.S. Metford appointed Instructor of Musketry at High Wycombe.	

Army Form C. 2118.

WAR DIARY
or
INTELLIGENCE SUMMARY.
(*Erase heading not required.*)

Instructions regarding War Diaries and Intelligence Summaries are contained in F. S. Regs., Part II. and the Staff Manual respectively. Title pages will be prepared in manuscript.

Place	Date	Hour	Summary of Events and Information	Remarks and references to Appendices
WHITTLE	26.		Sergt. Major Bishop Gazetted 2/Lieutenant.	
	28.		2 Officers and 9 N.C.Os. detailed to attend 10 days Musketry Course.	
			Cadet W.J.Rowden Gazetted 2/Lieutenant.	
			Ranging Board made and instruction commenced.	
	30.		Tactical Scheme Inspection by C.R.A.	

375

WAR DIARY.

Unit. 2/1st South Midland (Gloucestershire) Brigade R.F.A.

Division. 2/1st South Midland.

Mobilization Centre. Bristol.

Temporary War Station.

Stations since occupied subsequent to Concentration:-
Northampton.
Broomfield.
Writtle.

(a). **MOBILIZATION.** Nil.

(b). **CONCENTRATION AT WAR STATIONS.** (Including Railway Moves) NIL.

(c). **ORGANIZATION FOR DEFENCE.** (Including Vulnerable points) NIL.

(d). **TRAINING.** Steadily improving.

(e). **DISCIPLINE.** Good

(f). **ADMINISTRATION.**

    1. Medical Services.   Civilian Practitioner.

    2. Veterinary Services.   ~~Poor~~

    3. Supply Services.   Nil.

    4. Transport Services.   Nil.

    5. Ordnance Services.   Nil.

    6. Channels of Correspondence in Routine matters.   Nil.

    7. Billeting & Hutting.   Nil

    8. Range Construction.   Miniature Gun range constructed.

    9. Supply of Remounts.   Good. Stamp of horses satisfactory.

(g). RE-ORGANIZATION OF T-F. INTO HOME & IMPERIAL SERVICE.   Nil

(h). PREPARATION OF UNITS FOR IMPERIAL SERVICE.   Percentage of Inoculated men steadily rising.

STATION. Writtle, Essex.   Lieut. Colonel.

DATE. July 2nd 1915.   Commanding.

WAR DIARY
or
INTELLIGENCE SUMMARY

Army Form C. 2118

(Erase heading not required.)

Place	Date	Hour	Summary of Events and Information	Remarks and references to Appendices
	1915. July			
WRITTLE.	1st		Nine horses Cast and sold.	
	2nd	11.pm	Night Alarm. Brigade paraded on Village Green with Guns, Wagons etc, all ready to move off. Time:- half hour from alarm.	
	4th		Brigade take hot baths.	
CHELMSFORD	5th	5.45pm	Lecture by Mr Whitehead on Gunnery.	
MILL GREEN	5/6		Independent section operation by section of 3rd Battery under 2/Lieut.Rowden carried out, and inspected by the C.R.A.	
WRITTLE.	6th		Home Service men transferred to COLCHESTER.	
	7th		Competition for Trumpeters started.	
	8th		Corporal Stanley Longstaffe Dickinson, North Somerset Yeomanry gazetted 2/Lieutenant.	
	9th		All (50) .303 Rifles returned to Colchester.	
	10th		Major Dunscombe proceeds abroad on fortnights course at the Front. Class for Junior Officers started in Morse Code in early morning.	
	11th		2/Lieut. Ryder of 2/2nd S.M.Bde RFA attached for duty.	
	12th		3 officers and 9 N.C.O's attend 14 days Musketry Course.	
	12th		4 officers and 30 men Inoculated.	
	12th		Lance Sergeant Edgar Sidney Langdon Ostler, North Somerset Yeomanry gazetted 2/Lieutenant.	
	12/14	5.45		

Army Form C. 2118

WAR DIARY
or
INTELLIGENCE SUMMARY
(Erase heading not required.)

Instructions regarding War Diaries and Intelligence Summaries are contained in F.S. Regs., Part 2. and the Staff Manual respectively. Title Pages will be prepared in manuscript.

Place	Date 1915	Hour	Summary of Events and Information	Remarks and references to Appendices
WRITTLE	July 15/14th		Independent Section Operations by Section of 1st Battery under 2/Lieut. Ridler carried out, and Inspected by the C.R.A.	
	18.		Brigade ordered to move to INGATESTONE. Lieut. Lascelles appointed Billeting Officer vice Lieut. Noble.	
	19.		Move to INGATESTONE cancelled.	
	20.		75 Remount horses arrive for Brigade.	
	21.		Bivouac of one Battery at Screens Park.	
	22.		Brigade ordered to move to EPPING on July 26th 1915.	
	22.		Inspection of Camp by G.O.C.	
CHELMSFORD.	23.		Lecture by Major Austin on his Experiences at the Front.	
			Major Austin detailed as President of Court Martial.	
	24.		Major Hillman proceeds abroad on fortnights Course at the Front.	
EPPING.	26.		Brigade moves under Canvas at EPPING.	
			Ranging Board constructed by Commanding Officer.	
			Lieut. Bennett, A.V.C. attached to Brigade whilst at EPPING.	
			Sanitary Squad formed.	
	27.		25 men arrived from 3rd Line to be absorbed in our establishment.	

Stamp: Lt. S. MID. (GLOS.) 5 AUG 1915 F.A. BDE.

Army Form C. 2118

WAR DIARY
or
INTELLIGENCE SUMMARY
(Erase heading not required.)

Instructions regarding War Diaries and Intelligence Summaries are contained in F. S. Regs., Part II. and the Staff Manual respectively. Title Pages will be prepared in manuscript.

[Stamp: 2/1ST S. MID. (GLOS.) R.F.A. BDE. 5 AUG 1915]

Place	Date	Hour	Summary of Events and Information	Remarks and references to Appendices
EPPING.	1915 July 29th		Course of Map Reading under Lieut. Harris for Junior Officers and N.C.O's started.	
	30th		Lieut. Harris transferred from Ammunition Column to 2nd Battery.	

1875 Wt. W593/826 1,000,000 4/15 J.B.C. & A. A.D.S.S./Forms/C. 2118.

WAR DIARY.

Unit.   2/1st South Midland (Gloucestershire) Brigade R.F.A.

Division.   2/1st South Midland.

Mobilization Centre.   Bristol.

Temporary War Station.

Stations since occupied subsequent to Concentration:-
                                Northampton.
                                Broomfield.
                                Writtle.
                                Epping.

(a). MOBILIZATION.   Nil.

(b). CONCENTRATION AT WAR STATIONS. (Including Railway Moves) Nil.

(c). ORGANIZATION FOR DEFENCE. (Including Vulnerable Points) Nil.

(d). TRAINING.   Steadily improving.

(e). DISCIPLINE.   Good.

(f). ADMINISTRATION.

   1. Medical Services.   Poor.

   2. Veterinary Services. Good for time being (month under canvass)

   3. Supply Services.   Nil.

   4. Transport Services. Nil.

   5. Ordnance Services.   Nil.

   6. Channels of Correspondence
        in Routine matter. Nil.

   7. Billeting & Hutting. Nil.

   8. Range Construction.   Miniature Gun range constructed.

   9. Supply of Remounts.   Good. Stamp of horses satisfactory.

(g). RE-ORGANIZATION OF U.F. INTO HOME & IMPERIAL SERVICE.   Nil.

(h). PREPARATION OF UNIT FOR IMPERIAL SERVICE.   Percentage of Inoculated men steadily rising.

Station. Thornwood Camp, Epping.   Lieut.Colonel.
                                            Commanding.
Date.   5th August 1915.

Army Form C. 2118

WAR DIARY
or
INTELLIGENCE SUMMARY
(Erase heading not required.)

Instructions regarding War Diaries and Intelligence Summaries are contained in F. S. Regs., Part II and the Staff Manual respectively. Title Pages will be prepared in manuscript.

Place	Date 1915	Hour	Summary of Events and Information	Remarks and references to Appendices
EPPING	Augt 1st	9-50 a.m.	Church Parade	
	2nd		Bde Routine Order by Brig-Gen Daubeney, D.S.O. ordering 5 rounds of ammunition to be issued to each man of the Guard	
	3rd	6 a.m	Physical Drill commenced for Officers Clinton Gilbert McIlquham gazetted 2/Lieutenant, dated 16/7/15	
		5-30 a.m.	Reveille to be at 5 a.m. Stables & Physical Drill	
	5th		Brigade left EPPING at 8-45 a.m. for GREAT BADDOW and remained there for the night	
GT BADDOW	6th		Field Marshal Earl Kitchener inspected the Division in HYLANDS PARK at 11 a.m. Brigade returned to GREAT BADDOW for the night	
	7th		Brigade returns to Camp at EPPING	
EPPING	8th	9-50 a.m.	2/Lieuts Cope, S.A.Rowden, Unwin,Ellerton, Morgan, Ridler and W.H.Lanham to be Lieutenants Church Parade	
	9th		Lieut.Logan returns to duty and takes Command of 3rd Battery Major Austin attached to 2/2nd Bde as Instructor in Gunnery.	
	10th	6-15 a.m.	9 Drivers sent to 3rd Line to form part Nucleus Officers Riding Drill under R.S.M.	
	11th		Lieut.Cope granted 14 days sick leave	
	13th		Officers commenced to draw Rations	
	14th		Lieut.Noble took over duties as Adjutant	

Army Form C. 2118

WAR DIARY
or
INTELLIGENCE SUMMARY
(Erase heading not required.)

Instructions regarding War Diaries and Intelligence Summaries are contained in F.S. Regs., Part II. and the Staff Manual respectively. Title Pages will be prepared in manuscript.

Place	Date 1914	Hour	Summary of Events and Information	Remarks and references to Appendices
EPPING	Augt 14th		Bte.G.C.D.Fenwick A.O.C. gazetted 2/Lieutenant Brigade Order - B.C's to ensure all men having shower bath once a week.	
	15th	9-30 a.m.	Church Parade	
	16th		Corporal Cooks detailed to attend Saddlery Course. Capt.B.C.Biggar granted 10 days sick leave Major Langton T.Q.M.Stores, C.F. Inspected Messing system	
	17th		Major Austin returned to duty Major Hillman returned to duty, and to Command of 3rd Battery 1st Battery left this Brigade treking to GREAT BENTLY, bivouaced at GREAT BADDOW for the night	
		10-15 p.m.	Zeppelin passed over this Camp, came from S.E. and went S.W. Great Altitude, Infantry opened fire	
		10-30 p.m.	Report of Bombs heard in distance	
	18th		Pte C.A.Fenwick from H.A.C. gazetted 2/Lieutenant 2 Officers and 4 men inoculated.	
LEXDEN			1st Battery arrived at LEXDEN, Colchester and remained the night	
GREAT BENTLY EPPING	19th	2 p.m	1st Battery arrived at GREAT BENTLY Lieuts Ellerton & Ridler left for overseas Brigade Medical Inspection. M.O. reports Brigade in excellent health	
	20th	6-30 a.m.	Officers sword practice. Lieut Lindrea to be temporary Captain 2/Lieut.McIlquham granted sick leave indefinitely	
	21st		2/Lieut.G.C.D. Fenwick posted to Ammunition Column	

1875. Wt. W593/826 1,000,000 4/15 J.B.C. & A. A.D.S.S./Forms/C.2118.

Army Form C.2118

WAR DIARY
or
INTELLIGENCE SUMMARY
(Erase heading not required.)

Instructions regarding War Diaries and Intelligence Summaries are contained in F. S. Regs., Part II. and the Staff Manual respectively. Title Pages will be prepared in manuscript.

Place	Date 1915	Hour	Summary of Events and Information	Remarks and references to Appendices
EPPING	Augt 21st		Major Dunscombe granted 14 days sick leave. Skeleton Tactical Scheme under Brig-Gen Daubeney, D.S.O. Officers present, Lt.Col.F.K.S.Metford, Major Hillman, Lieut.Harris and Capt.James	
	22nd	9-30 a.m.	Church parade	
			Capt.C.K.S.Metford dated 30/7/15 and Capt.J.P.Jenkins dated 13/7/15, seconded for duty at the Artillery Training School, Kettering. 2/Lieut.E.S.L.Ostler appointed Brigade Orderly Officer	
	23rd		3rd Battery Section Bivouac on Luton Common	
	26th		Field operations under Brig-Gen E.K.Daubeney, D.S.O. in which Whole Brigade took part. General Staff and R.A.Staff 61st Division, present 2/Lieuts C.A. & G.C.D.Fenwick reported for duty.	
GT.BENTLY	27th		1st Battery left GREAT BENTLY. Remained night at LEXDEN.	
EPPING			Medical Board held on men physically unfit for F.S. Medical Inspection of men under 18. Medical Inspection of all Officers	
GT.BADDOW	28th		1st Battery arrived at GREAT BADDOW	
EPPING	29th		1st Battery remained at GREAT BADDOW Examination for promotion to Corporals and Sergeants	
	30th		1st Battery arrived at EPPING 2nd Battery Section Bivouac Capt.B.C.Biggar returned to duty	
	31st		Capt.B.C.Biggar posted to 3rd Battery 1 Officer and 14 men inoculated	

WAR DIARY.

Unit- 2/1st South Midland (Gloucestershire) Brigade RFA

Division- 2/1st South Midland.

Mobilization Centre. Bristol.

Temporary War Station.

Stations since occupied subsequent to Concentration:-

    Northampton,
    Broomfield,
    Writtle,
    Epping.

(a) MOBILIZATION.   Nil.

(b) CONCENTRATION AT WAR STATIONS. (Including Railway Moves) Nil.

(c) ORGANIZATION FOR DEFENCE. (Including Vulnerable Points) XXX

    1st Battery at Great Bently from August 19-27

(d) TRAINING.   Steadily Improving.

(e) DISCIPLINE.   Good.

(f) ADMINISTRATION)

    1. Medical Services.   Good.

    2. Veterinary Services.   Good.

    3. Supply Services.   Good.

    4. Transport Services.   Good.

    5. Ordnance Services.   Nil.

    6. Channels of Correspondence in Routine matter.   Nil.

    7. Billeting & Hutting.   Nil.

    8. Range Construction.   Miniature Gun range contruction improving.

    9. Supply of Remounts.   Nil.

(g) PREPARATION OF UNITS FOR IMPERIAL SERVICE. Inoculated Officers and men nearly 100%

Station. Thornwood Camp, Epping

Date, 34? September 1915.

Lieut. Colonel.
Commanding.

W A R   D I A R Y.

Unit-   2/1st South Midland (Gloucestershire) Brigade RFA
Division-   2/1st South Midland.
Mobilization Centre.   Bristol.
Temporary War Station.
Stations since occupied subsequent to Concentration:-
                            Northampton,
                            Broomfield,
                            Writtle,
                            Epping.

(a) MOBILIZATION.   Nil.

(b) CONCENTRATION AT WAR STATIONS.(Including Railway Moves) Nil.

(c) ORGANIZATION FOR DEFENCE.(Including Vulnerable Points) XXX.
        1st Battery at Great Bently from August 19-27.

(d) TRAINING.   Steadily Improving.

(e) DISCIPLINE.   Good.

(f) ADMINISTRATION)

    1. Medical Services.   Good.
    2. Veterinary Services.   Good.
    3. Supply Services.   Good.
    4. Transport Services.   Good.
    5. Ordnance Services.   Nil.
    6. Channels of Correspondence
       in Routine matters.   Nil.
    7. Billeting & Hutting.   Nil.
    8. Range Construction.   Miniature Gun range contruction
                                 improving.
    9. Supply of Remounts.   Nil.

(g) PREPARATION OF UNITS FOR IMPERIAL SERVICE. Inoculated Officers
                                               and men nearly
                                               100%.

                                    Lieut. Colonel.
                                    Commanding.

Station. Thornwood Camp,
         Epping

Date 3rd September, 1915.

Army Form C. 2118.

WAR DIARY
or
INTELLIGENCE SUMMARY.
(Erase heading not required.)

305 Bde R.F.A

Place	Date	Hour	Summary of Events and Information	Remarks and references to Appendices
EPPING	1915 Sept 2nd		Hay Nets brought into use	ayu
	3rd		19 recruits arrived from 3rd Line and posted to Ammn Col. Weekly Brigade Medical Inspection Major Dunscombe 14 days extension of sick leave. Advance party proceeded to INGATESTONE for change of Station.	ayu
	4th		Brigade moved to INGATESTONE. Left EPPING 6 a.m. arrived INGATESTONE 2 p.m. by road.	ayu
INGATE-STONE	5th		New Medical Officer - Lt.Hutchinson. Horse sanatorium for poor horses arranged.	ayu
	6th	6 a.m	Subaltern Officers attended Stables and groomed their own Horses. Horses fed 4 times daily. 7 a.m. 12 noon 4 p.m. 8 p.m.	ayu
	7th		C.R.A. visited the Camp. 52 Horses taken over from 2/4th S.M. (H) Bde, R.F.A. G.O.C. visited the Camp. Lt.Col.F.K.S.Metford attended Court Martial at Chelmsford for instruction. Zeppelin observed going towards London at 11.15 p.m.	ayu
	9th		Brigade Supply Train commenced, proceeding to Chelmsford at 8.30 a.m. daily. 5 days leave with free travelling Warrant commenced.	ayu
	11th		Zeppelin dropped bombs on late Camp at EPPING	ayu
	12th		2/Lieut.P.T.Rowe commenced Gunnery Course at Shoeburyness on 15 & 18 prs	ayu
	14th	10 a.m	Brigade inspected in "The Field" by the C.R.A. Precautions taken against observation by Hostile Aircraft. Horse lines moved under hedges. Tents ditto. Commenced painting Tents	ayu

Army Form C. 2118.

WAR DIARY
or
INTELLIGENCE SUMMARY.

(Erase heading not required.)

Instructions regarding War Diaries and Intelligence Summaries are contained in F.S. Regs., Part II. and the Staff Manual respectively. Title pages will be prepared in manuscript.

Place	Date	Hour	Summary of Events and Information	Remarks and references to Appendices
INGATE-STONE	1915 Sept 14th		2 Recruits arrived from Admin. Centre and posted to 1st Battery. Working Men's Club opened for recreation in INGATESTONE	
	15th		81 Remounts arrived. Good class L.D. Ammunition Column Section Bivouac at MILL GREEN	
	16th		2 Recruits arrived from Admin.Centre and posted to 1st Battery	
	17th		7 Cast Horses sold at Chelmsford. Average price £16.14.6. Instructions received re placing of Guns for attack on Zeps. 14 days extension of sick leave granted to Major Dunscombe.	
	20th		Veterinary Officer lectures to all Officers.	
	21st		Zep trap ready. Map reading class for N.C.O's re-commenced.	
	23rd		Redrilling of N.C.O's by R.S.M. at 6.15 a.m. each morning commenced. Village of FELSTED placed out of bounds through outbreak of Diphtheria. Instructions received re Munitions Workers	
	25th		2nd Line Transport inspected by Col.Collis, A.S.C. Brigade Medical Inspection.	
		2 p.m	Brigade Sports held.	
	26th		Army Acts 4 – 15 and 9 – 22 read out to Brigade Parade	
	27th		8 N.C.O's arrived from 8th Provisional Battn for instruction in 90 m/m Gun drill.	
	28th		5 Horses (Vice) to Romford Remount Depot. 2/Lascelles 4 days sick leave. 14 men sent to Home Service.	

1577 Wt.W10791/1773 500,000 1/15 D.D.&L. A.D.S.S./Forms/C. 2118.

WAR DIARY or INTELLIGENCE SUMMARY

Army Form C. 2118.

Place	Date	Hour	Summary of Events and Information	Remarks and references to Appendices
INGATESTONE	1915. Sept 30th		Brigade Parade addressed by Sir George Croydon M.P. - Marks, representative of Minister of Munitions. Medical Board at Chelmsford. 1 man for Home Service Driver Rossiter 2nd Battery attaends school of Cookery, Middlewick for instruction.	

FkSmithe Lt. Colonel,
Commanding
2/1st S. Midland (Glo'ster)

Army Form C. 2118.

WAR DIARY
or
INTELLIGENCE SUMMARY.
(Erase heading not required.)

Instructions regarding War Diaries and Intelligence Summaries are contained in F. S. Regs., Part II and the Staff Manual respectively. Title pages will be prepared in manuscript.

Place	Date	Hour	Summary of Events and Information	Remarks and references to Appendices
EPPING	1915 Sept 2nd		Hay Nets brought into use	
	3rd		19 recruits arrived from 3rd Line and posted to A'mmn Col. Major Dunscombe 14 days extension of sick leave. Advance party proceeded to INGATESTONE for change of station.	Weekly Brigade Medical Inspection
	4th		Brigade moved to INGATESTONE. Left EPPING 6 a.m. arrived INGATESTONE 2 p.m. by road.	
INGATE-STONE	5th 6th	6 a.m	New Medical Officer - Lt.Hutchinson. Horse sanatorium for poor horses arranged. Subaltern Officers attended Stables and groomed their own horses. Horses fed 4 times daily. C.R.A. visited the Camp. 52 Horses taken over from 2/4th S.M. (H) Bde, R.F.A.	7 a.m. 12 noon 4 p.m. 7 p.m.
	7th		G.O.C. visited the Camp. Lt.Col.F.K.S.Metford attended Court Martial at Chelmsford for instruction. Zeppelin observed going towards London at 11.15 p.m.	
	9th		Brigade Supply Train commenced, proceeding to Chelmsford at 8.30 a.m. daily. with free travelling Warrant commenced.	5 days leave
	11th		Zeppelin dropped bombs on late Camp at EPPING	
	12th		2/Lieut.P.T.Rowe commenced Gunnery Course at Shoeburyness on 15 & 18 prs	
	14th	10 a.m	Brigade inspected in "The Field" by the C.R.A. Precautions taken against observation by Hostile Aircraft. Horse lines moved under hedges. Tents ditto. Commenced painting Tents	

Army Form C. 2118.

WAR DIARY
or
INTELLIGENCE SUMMARY.

(Erase heading not required.)

Instructions regarding War Diaries and Intelligence Summaries are contained in F. S. Regs., Part II. and the Staff Manual respectively. Title pages will be prepared in manuscript.

Place	Date	Hour	Summary of Events and Information	Remarks and references to Appendices
INGATE-STONE	1915 Sept 14th		2 Recruits arrived from Admin. Centre and posted to 1st Battery. Working Men's Club opened for recreation in INGATESTONE	
	15th		31 Remounts arrived. Good class L.D. Ammunition Column Section Bivouac at MILL GREEN	
	16th		2 Recruits arrived from Admin.Centre and posted to 1st Battery	
	17th		7 Cast Horses sold at Chelmsford. Average price £16.14.6. Instructions received re placing of Guns for attack on Zeps. 14 days extension of sick leave granted to Major Dunscombe.	
	20th		Veterinary Officer lectures to all Officers.	
	21st		Zep trap ready. Map reading class for N.C.O's re-commenced.	
	23rd		Redrilling of N.C.O's by R.S.M. at 6.15 a.m. each morning commenced. Village of FELSTED. Placed out of bounds through outbreak of Diphtheria. Instructions received re Munitions Workers	
	25th		2nd Line Transport inspected by Col.Collis, A.S.C. Brigade Medical Inspection.	
	26th	2 p.m	Brigade Sports held.	
			Army Acts 4 - 15 and 9 - 22 read out to Brigade Parade	
	27th		3 N.C.O's arrived from 8th Provisional Battn for instruction in 90 m/m Gun drill.	
	28th		5 Horses (Vice) to Romford Remount Depot. 2/Lascelles 4 days sick leave.	
			14 men sent to Home Service.	

Army Form C. 2118.

WAR DIARY
or
INTELLIGENCE SUMMARY.
(Erase heading not required.)

Instructions regarding War Diaries and Intelligence Summaries are contained in F. S. Regs., Part II. and the Staff Manual respectively. Title pages will be prepared in manuscript.

Place	Date	Hour	Summary of Events and Information	Remarks and references to Appendices
INGATESTONE	1915. Sept 30th		Brigade Parade addressed by Sir — Marks, representative of Minister of Munitions. Medical Board at Chelmsford. 1 man for Home Service Driver Rossiter 2nd Battery attends School of Cookery, Middlewick for instruction.	

WAR DIARY.

Unit. 2/1st South Midland (Gloucestershire) Brigade, R.F.A.

Division. 61st (South Midland)

Mobilization Centre   Bristol

Temporary War Station.

Stations since occupied subsequent to Concentration:-
         Northampton
         Broomfield
         Writtle
         Epping.
         Ingatestone

(a) MOBILIZATION   Nil

(b) CONCENTRATION AT WAR STATIONS (Including Railway Moves) Nil

(c) ORGANIZATION FOR DEFENCE (Including Vulnerable Points) Nil

(d) Training   Steadily improving.

(e) DISCIPLINE   Very good

(f) ADMINISTRATION

     1. Medical Services   Good.

     2. Veterinary Services   Good

     3. Supply Services   Good

     4. Transport Services   Good

     5. Ordnance Services   Nil

     6. Channels of Correspondence in Routine matter   Nil

     7. Billeting & Hutting   Nil

     8. Range Construction   New large Miniature Gun Range constructed at new Station.

     9. Supply of Remounts   Good.

(g) PREPARATION OF UNITS FOR IMPERIAL SERVICE. Inoculated Officers & Men nearly 100%

STATION   THE CAMP, INGATESTONE, ESSEX

DATE   5th OCTOBER, 1915.

                       Lt. Colonel
                       Commanding

WAR DIARY
or
INTELLIGENCE SUMMARY

(Erase heading not required.)

Army Form C.2118

Instructions regarding War Diaries and Intelligence Summaries are contained in F.S. Regs., Part II. and the Staff Manual respectively. Title Pages will be prepared in manuscript.

Place	Date	Hour	Summary of Events and Information	Remarks and references to Appendices
INGATESTONE	1915 Oct 1st		Lieut.Noble, A.G. to be Adjutant (August 20th)	
	4th		1 Cast Horse sold at Chelmsford. 13 men vaccinated(1st Batch) 2/Lt.Lascelles granted 4 days extension of sick leave. 21 Boxes of S.A.A transferred to 2/5th East Kent Regt. C.R.A. inspected Officers Buzzer Class	
	5th	5 pm	W.H.Friend to be 2/Lieutenant. Posted to Ammunition Column. Brigade Tactical Scheme Highwood and Mill Green. Conference by C.R.A. for Officers, Staff Sergts and Sergeants 2/Lt.Lascelles granted further extension of sick leave.	
	6th		15 Boxes of S.A.A. transferred to 2/5th East Kent Regt. Inoculation - 4 Officers 17 men. 59 Munition workers interviewed by skilled investigator Mr.Ead, 24 of whom were not passed. Ammunition loading time test from Brigade Magazine. 12 Recruits arrived and posted 4 to 1st Battery 4 to 2nd Bty and 4 to Ammn Column.	
	7th		25 Riding Horses received "on loan" from 2/2nd S.M.Bde, R.F.A.	
	8th		4 men vaccinated. 13 Recruits arrived and posted 6 to 3rd Battery and 7 to 2nd Battery B.Q.M.S. Nurse to be 2/Lieutenant and posted to Ammunition Column. 2/Lt.Lascelles granted 7 days extension of sick leave	
	9th		1 Recruit arrived and posted to 1st Battery.	
	11th 12th		3 Recruits arrived and posted to 1st Battery. 3rd Battery inspected by C.O.Bde in Drill Order 15 Recruits arrived and posted 5 to 1st Battery, 5 to 2nd Battery and 5 to 3rd Battery Lieutenant Noble A.G. to be Captain and remain Adjutant. Lieutenant Harris, E.S. to be Captain Brigade took part in Divisional Tactical Exercises Witham - Wickam Bishops.	
	12/13th 13th		24 L.D.Horses (Remounts) arrived from Romsey. Zeppelin raid on London. Zeps passed near Camp G.H.Pearson to be 2/Lieutenant and posted to 2nd Battery	Appendix No.1

1875 Wt. W593/826 1,000,000 4/15 J.B.C. & A. A.D.S.S./Forms/C.2118.

WAR DIARY
or
INTELLIGENCE SUMMARY

(Erase heading not required.)

Army Form C. 2118

Place	Date	Hour	Summary of Events and Information	Remarks and references to Appendices
INGATE-STONE	Oct 14th		District Court Martial on 2496 Driver Cambell, J. at Saracen's Head Hotel, Chelmsford. Awarded 21 days Detention, from 16th October. Bombr.Hadgson attends Course of Signalling at 3rd Army, Dunmow for 6 weeks Major Dunscombe attends Medical Board at Boreham House. 2/Lieutenant P.T.Rowe transferred from A.C. to 1st Battery.	
	15th		17 Recruits arrived and posted 10 to Ammunition Columnand 7 to 3rd Battery 123 Riding Horses arrived from 2/2nd S.W.Mtd Brigade, Colchester. Segregation found necessary Very poor condition. Cases of mange etc.	
	16th		Lieut.D.P.Morgan embarks for France.	
	17th		2/Lieutenants Rowden, W.J. and Fenwick, G.C.D. attends course at No.3 T.F.Artillery Training School, Kettering. 6/10 weeks.	
	18th		Medical Board at Chelmsford. 4 men attended	
	19/21st		Brigade took part in Divisional Manoeuvres. Witham - Tiptree - Wickam Bishops.	Appendix No 2
	20th		16 Jap Carbines transferred to 2/1st S.M.R.G.A.	
	22nd		Medical Board. 1 man attended	
	23rd		Gunner Hicks, F. No.2208 awarded 28 days Detention by C.O.Brigade	
	24th	5.30 p.m.	O.R.A. inspected the 123 Horses	
			Lt.Col F.K.S.Metford and Major Hillman attends Refresher Course at Shoeburyness.	
	25th		2271 S/Smith Ball, EM sentenced to 14 days Detention by C.O. Brigade moved into Billets	
	27th	2.30	2/Lieutenant Fielding, J.C. attends course at Edinburgh University 4 weeks Major Austin, Major Dunscombe and Capt.Noble attended lecture by G.O.C. at Shire Hall, Chelmsford on Courts Martial	

Army Form C. 2118

WAR DIARY
or
INTELLIGENCE SUMMARY
(Erase heading not required.)

Instructions regarding War Diaries and Intelligence Summaries are contained in F. S. Regs., Part II. and the Staff Manual respectively. Title Pages will be prepared in manuscript.

Place	Date	Hour	Summary of Events and Information	Remarks and references to Appendices
INGATE-STONE	1915 Oct 28th		Inoculation 12 men	
	29th		Inoculation 18 men	
			Brigade took part in Tactical Scheme under Sir John Barnsley 183rd Infantry Brigade Mountnessing - Hutton - Shenfield	Appendix A.63
	30th		Div.Authority to use War Establishment Part IX T.F. 2nd Line. 1915	
			Strength of Brigade at this date:- 30 Officers, 648 men and 542 Horses.	
			******************************	

1875 Wt. W593/826 1,000,000 4/15 J.B.C. & A. A.D.S.S./Forms/C. 2118.

Army Form C. 2118

WAR DIARY
or
INTELLIGENCE SUMMARY
(Erase heading not required.)

Instructions regarding War Diaries and Intelligence Summaries are contained in F. S. Regs., Part II. and the Staff Manual respectively. Title Pages will be prepared in manuscript.

Place	Date	Hour	Summary of Events and Information	Remarks and references to Appendices
INGATESTONE	1915 Oct 1st		Lieut.Noble, A.G. to be Adjutant (August 30th)	Appendix No 1
	4th		1 Cast Horse sold at Chelmsford. 13 men vaccinated(1st Batch) 2/Lt.Lascelles granted 4 days extension of sick leave. 21 Boxes of S.A.A transferred to 2/5th East Kent Regt. C.R.A. Inspected Officers Buzzer Class	Appendix No 2
	5th	5 pm	W.H.Friend to be 2/Lieutenant. Posted to Ammunition Column. Brigade Tactical Scheme Highwood and Mill Green. Conference by C.R.A. for Officers, Staff Sergts 'd Sergeants 2/Lt.Lascelles granted further extension of sick leave.	Appendix No 3
	6th		15 Boxes of S.A.A. transferred to 2/5th East Kent Regt. Inoculation - 4 Officers 17 men. 59 Munition workers interviewed by skilled investigator Mr.Ead, 24 of whom were not passed. Ammunition loading time test from Brigade Magazine. 12 Recruits arrived and posted 4 to 1st Battery 4 to 2nd Bty and 4 to Amsn Column.	
	7th		25 Riding Horses received "on loan" from 2/2nd E.M.Bde, R.F.A.	
	8th		4 men vaccinated. 15 Recruits arrived and posted 6 to 3rd Battery and 7 to 2nd Battery B.Q.M.S. Nuree to be 2/Lieutenant and posted to Ammunition Column. 2/Lt.Lascelles granted 7 days extension of sick leave	
	9th		1 Recruit arrived and posted to 1st Battery.	
	11th 12th		5 Recruits arrived and posted to 1st Battery. 3rd Battery Inspected by G.O.C.Bde in Drill Order 15 Recruits arrived and posted 5 to 1st Battery, 5 to 2nd Battery and 5 to 3rd Battery Lieutenant Holm;A.G. to be Captain and remain Adjutant. Lieutenant Harris, E.S. to be Captain	
	12/13th		Brigade took part in Divisional Tactical Exercises Witham - Wickam Bishops.	
	15th		24 L.D.Horses (Remounts) arrived from Romsey. Zeppelin raid on London. Zeps passed near Camp G.H.Pearson to be 2/Lieutenant and posted to 2nd Battery	

Army Form C. 2118

WAR DIARY
or
INTELLIGENCE SUMMARY

(Erase heading not required.)

Instructions regarding War Diaries and Intelligence Summaries are contained in F. S. Regs., Part II. and the Staff Manual respectively. Title Pages will be prepared in manuscript.

Place	Date	Hour	Summary of Events and Information	Remarks and references to Appendices
INGATE-STONE	Oct 14th		District Court Martial on 2496 Driver Cambell, J. at Saracen's Head Hotel, Chelmsford. Awarded 21 days Detention, from 16th October. Bombr.Hadgson attends Course of Signalling at 3rd Army, Dunmow for 6 weeks Major Dunscombe attends Medical Board at Boreham House. 2/Lieutenant P.T.Rowe transferred from A.C. to 1st Battery.	
	15th		17 Recruits arrived and posted to Ammunition Columnand 7 to 3rd Battery 123 Riding Horses arrived from 2/2nd S.W.Mtd Brigade, Colchester. Segregation found necessary. Very poor condition. Cases of mange etc.	
	16th		Lieut.D.P.Morgan embarks for France.	
	17th		2/Lieutenants Rowden, W.J. and Fenwick, G.C.D. attends course at No.3 T.F.Artillery Training School, Kettering. 6/10 weeks.	
	13th		Medical Board at Chelmsford. 4 men attended	
	19/21st		Brigade took part in Divisional Manoeuvres. Witham - Tiptree - Wickam Bishops.	
	20th		16 Jap Carbines transferred to 2/1st S.M.R.G.A.	
	22nd		Medical Board. 1 man attended	
	23rd		Gunner Hicks, F. No.2208 awarded 28 days Detention by C.O.Brigade	
	24th	5.30 p.m.	C.R.A. inspected the 123 Horses	
			Lt.Col F.K.S.Metford and Major Hillman attends Refresher Course at Shoeburyness.	
	25th		2271 S/Smith Ball, EM sentenced to 14 days Detention by C.O. Brigade moved into Billets	
	27th	2.30	2/Lieutenant Fielding, J.C. attends course at Edinburgh University 4 weeks Major Austin, Major Dunscombe and Capt.Noble attended lecture by G.O.C. at Shire Hall, Chelmsford on Courts Martial	

Army Form C. 2118

WAR DIARY
or
INTELLIGENCE SUMMARY
(Erase heading not required.)

Instructions regarding War Diaries and Intelligence Summaries are contained in F. S. Regs., Part II. and the Staff Manual respectively. Title Pages will be prepared in manuscript.

Place	Date	Hour	Summary of Events and Information	Remarks and references to Appendices
INGATE-STONE	1915 Oct 28th		Inoculation 12 men	
	29th		Inoculation 18 men. Brigade took part in Tactical Scheme under Sir John Barnsley 183rd Infantry Brigade - Hutton - Shenfield Mountnessing -	
	30th		Div. Authority to use War Establishment Part IX T.F. 2nd Line. 1915 Strength of Brigade at this date:- 30 Officers, 648 men and 542 Horses.	

****

WAR DIARY

Unit. 2/1st South Midland (Gloucestershire) Brigade, R.F.A.

Division. 61st (South Midland)

Mobilization Centre Bristol

Temporary War Station

Stations since occupied subsequent to Concentration:-

                                                 Northampton
                                                 Broomfield
                                                 Writtle
                                                 Epping (Canvas)
                                                 Ingatestone (Canvas)
                                                 Ingatestone (Billets)

(a) **MOBILIZATION**   Nil

(b) **CONCENTRATION AT WAR STATIONS** (Including Railway Moves) Nil

(c) **ORGANIZATION FOR DEFENCE** (Including Vulnerable Points) Nil

(d) **TRAINING** Steadily improving.

(e) **DISCIPLINE** Very Good

(f) **ADMINISTRATION**

     1. Medical Services   Good

     2. Veterinary Services   Good

     3. Supply Services   Good

     4. Transport Services   Good

     5. Ordnance Services   Nil

     6. Channels of correspondence Nil
         in Routine matters

     7. Billeting and Hutting   Fairly Good

     8. Range Construction   Nil

     9. Supply of Remounts   Good

(g) **PREPARATION OF UNITS FOR IMPERIAL SERVICE**   Inoculated Officers and men nearly 100%

STATION   INGATESTONE, ESSEX

DATE   3rd NOVEMBER. 1915

                                                   Captain
                                                   Adjutant
                                                   Major
                                                   Commanding

2/1st SOUTH MIDLAND (GLOUCESTERSHIRE) BRIGADE, R.F.A.

WAR DIARY

Appendix No. 1.

SUMMARY OF DIVISIONAL TACTICAL SCHEME

which took place on October 12-13th, 1915

WITHAM - WICKHAM BISHOPS

Orders sent out.	Orders received.
Message to R.A. Headquarters HATFIELD GREEN at 4.50 p.m. 12/10/15 saying refilling point of this Brigade FORKED ROAD-RAILWAY BRIDGE below BERTON HALL	Divisional Order No. 1. 9/10/15 General Idea. Division will occupy trench line HEYBRIDGE to CHIPPINGHILL on Tuesday 12/10/15. C.R.A. will detail the Artillery for each section of the defence. General Reserve at HATFIELD PEVEREL. Refilling Point HATFIELD PEVEREL. Divl HdQrs at THE PRIORY S.W. of HATFIELD GREEN.
Artillery Orders No. 1 Issued to Battery Commanders from WITHAM at 12 noon 12/10/15. Position of Batteries:- Left Battery (1st) at hedge running through second "P" in CHIPPING-HILL. Centre Battery (2nd) "T" in LARGE WITHAM Right Battery (3rd) at last "S" in ISHAM'S FARM. Detail:- Capt. James will act as Conducting Officer over Rations and report to A.S.C. at HATFIELD PEVEREL at 7.30 p.m. Reports to Brigade HdQrs as soon as position is taken up, by Motor Cyclist Orderly. Battery Commanders to notify his Observation Station to the Infantry Commanders in front of his Battery position.	Sketch received showing A.S.C. and R. . Transport and refilling point.
	Artillery Order No.1. 11/10/15. Detail of Artillery. 2/1st S.M. Bde, R.F.A. is detailed for No. 2 Section of Defence and will be clear of COLCHESTER ROAD-CHELMSFORD HIGH STREET CORNER, by 10.15 a.m. marching via HATFIELD PEVEREL and WITHAM. Divisional Artillery HdQrs will open at WHEATSHEAF INN, HATFIELD GREEN at 3.45 p.m. on 12/10/15 Issued at 6.50 p.m. 11/10/15
Message to Left Battery sent at 7.25 p.m. from WICKHAM BISHOPS 12/10/15. HdQrs R.A. decide your Battery is too much in open. Take up another position at dawn at least 400/500 yds right or left of present epaulments. One section to be moved at a time and report when completed. If possible a further back should be taken as Infantry only 726 yds in front.	Letter from Headquarters, R.A. giving particulars of method to be employed in the supply of rations.
	Operation Order No.1. 184 Inf Bde Enemy (White Hat Bands) in direction of Colchester. Strength unknown. Intention to hold existing line of entrenchments. Disposition of Infantry. Fires & Cooking:- No fires will be visible from the front. Dressing Station in vicinity of Headquarters. Reports to Brigade HdQrs at WICKHAM BISHOP'S P.O.
Message to Centre Battery sent at 7.25 p.m. from WICKHAM BISHOPS 12/10/15. HdQrs R.A. decide your Battery too much in open, and must be moved 400/500 yds Right or left of present epaulments at dawn, to draw enemy's fire if possible insert dummy guns. Guns to be throughly concealed and report when completed. One section at a time to be moved.	Letter from R.A. HdQrs saying the D.A.C. is imaginary. Road (rail) is CHELMSFORD. Rendezvous is road triangle at LITTLE BADDOW

Orders sent out

Message to HdQrs 182 Inf Bde sent at 7.30 p.m. from WICKHAM BISHOPS 12/10/15:- Ammunition Column of this Brigade is at FORKED ROAD, RAILWAY CROSSING immediately S of BRENTON HALL on halfinch map.

Message to Howitzer Battery sent at 7.50 a.m. from WICKHAM BISHOPS 13/10/15:- C.R.A. informs us that Brigade General Bowes will inspect all Gun positions to-day. Inform Heavy Battery.

Message to Heavy Battery sent at 7.50 a.m. from WICKHAM BISHOPS 13/10/15;- C.R.A. informs us that BRIGADE General Bowes will inspect all Gun position to-day. Please inform Howitzer Battery.

Message to HdQrs R.A. sent at 7.30 a.m. from WICKHAM BISHOPS 13/10/15:- Asking for nature and position of Guns on our left.

Message to all Batteries sent at 8.45 a.m. from WICKHAM BISHOPS 13/10/15:- Advise Infantry position on your Observing Station for purpose of Communication.

Advising R.A.hqrs of Battery positions. Sent at 8.25 a.m. from WICKHAM BISHOPS, 13/10/15 Ref 6" map. Left Bty position at 7.20 a.m. this morning:-Old gun Epaulments N of R.C.Church at WITHAM.
Centre Battery new position at 7 a.m. 300 yds W of BARN GROVE in Hedge.
Right Battery unaltered.
Communication between Brigade Commanders and B.C's:- Motor Cyclist.
Asking for nature and position of guns on right flank.

Message to Battery Commanders sent at 9.15 a.m. from WICKHAM BISHOPS 13/10/15, asking for Range Tables from new positions.

Advising R.A.HdQrs of Battery position. Sent at 9.30 a.m. from WICKHAM BISHOPS 13/10/15. Centre Battery new position 1½" N of ISHAM'S FARM at termination of foot path in BARN GROVE

Communication from 2/5th Glosters asking for position of observers near their trenches.
Sent from BROOMFIELD FARM 8.50a.m. 13/10/15.

Message from 184th Bde received at 9. Graces becomes falling sick to stay on ff side of the road and report to Officer i/c Ambulance. No other than the driver to ride on any wagon.

Message from 184th Inf Bde. 11.40am 13/10/15.
Cyclist patrol sighted enemy point 180 road TIPTREE to PRIORY. 10.30 a.m.

Letter from HdQrs R.A. at HATFIELD GREEN 13/10/15 requesting position of A.C. One sketch(panorama) by each Battery to reach them by 4 p.m. Communication with observing posts must be by telephone. Field States to reach them daily by noon.

Message from R.A. HdQrs HATFIELD GREEN 13/10/15. Veterinary receiving station for Batteries N of line LANGFORD GROVE, LITTLE TOTHAM HALL, is the CROWN HOTEL HATFIELD PEVEREL.
Horse casualties occurring S of this line are to be conveyed by train from MALDON to the Veterinary Hospital, CHELMSFORD

Communication from 184th Inf Bde 2.22 p.m. 13/10/15.
182nd Inf Bde report enemy's scouts all along their line. Enemy cavalry strength 2 Squadrons reported in GOLDHANGER.

Message from 2/5th Glosters to 3rd Battery. 2.7 p.m. from BROOMFIELD FARM. 13/10/15.
One Company of enemy infantry reported resting on COLCHESTER WITHAM road.½mile N.E. of RIVENHALL end. Ref sheet 30 ½" map.

Message from Brigade Major R.A. WHEATSHEAF INN, HATFIELD GREEN 3.50 p.m. 13/10/15.

Troops will proceed home at 5 p.m.

Orders sent out	Orders received.

To O.C. Right Battery 12.10 p.m.
WICKHAM BISHOPS 13/10/15.
  Infantry reports enemy scouts at
point 180 ½ mile S.W. of CHURCH at
TIPTREE 1" map at 10.30 a.m.

  To all Batteries. 1.30 p.m. 13/10/15
WICKHAM BISHOPS. Forward panorama
sketch at once.

  Letter to R.A.HdQrs 13/10/15 WICKHAM
BISHOPS.
  A.C. facing fork of Road S of BENTON
HALL 1 mile S of WITHAM

  All Batteries connected to Observation
Post by telephone.
  Field States already sent.

  Letter to R.A.HdQrs 13/10/15 from
WICKHAM BISHOPS.
  Horses passed by A.D.V.S. as
follows:-
    1st Bty Fair 2nd Bty Good
3rd Bty Good.

  Message to R.A.HdQrs 13/10/15
WICKHAM BISHOPS 2.15 p.m.
Copies of reports from Batteries
sent. Panorama sketches to follow.

  To all Batteries 13/10/15
WICKHAM BISHOPS 2.45 p.m.
  182nd Inf Bde report enemy scouts
all along their line. Enemy cavalry
strength 2 Squadrons reported in
GOLDHANGER.

  To Left Battery 13/10/15 3 p.m.
WICKHAM BISHOPS.
  2/5th Glosters report enemy Inf
resting on WITHAM-COLCHESTER ROAD
¼ mile N.E. of RIVENHALL END. Ref
sheet 30.

  Message to 2/5th Glosters 13/10/15
3.7 p.m. WICKHAM BISHOPS.
  3rd Battery HALES FARM. Have
instructed Left Battery at WITHAM
to fire on enemy.

  Message to R.A.HdQrs from WICKHAM
BISHOPS 3.45 p.m. 13/10/15.
  Major Austin Cmdg Left Bty
temporary casualty.

  Message to R.A.HdQrs. WICKHAM
BISHOPS 3.50 p.m. 13/10/15.
Sending panorama sketches. Company of
Inf reported resting on WITHAM-
COLCHESTER ROAD ¼ mile N.E. of RIVENHALL
END. Instructed Left Bty to fire.

Orders sent out.	Orders received.

Message to all Batteries
WICKHAM BISHOPS 15/10/16.
4.20 p.m.

Prepare to move in direction
of IRKA ESTORE at once.

Starting point Cr ss Roads
WICKHAM BISHOPS- TIPTRE.
Starting time 5.15 p.m.

============

Appendix No. 2.

WAR DIARY -OR- INTELLIGENCE SUMMARY.

2/1ST SOUTH MIDLAND (GLOUCESTERSHIRE) BRIGADE R.F.A.

DIVISIONAL MANOEUVRES October 19–20–21st. WITHAM – TIPTREE – WICKHAM BISHOPS

Brigade left INGATESTONE 19/10/15. S. P. GRANGEMOUNT. S.T. 8.30.a.m. in order as follows:-

Brigade Headquarters Staff.

1st Battery. 2. Guns. 3. Ammunition Wagons.
2nd Battery. 4. Guns. 4. Ammunition Wagons.
3rd Battery. 4. Guns. 4. Ammunition Wagons.
Headquarters. 1. Supply Wagon. 1. Red Cross Wagon.
1st Battery. 3. Supply Wagons. }
2nd Battery. 3. Supply Wagons. } 6 S A A
3rd Battery. 3. Supply Wagons. 4 G.S. Wagons. (Amm.Column men and horses)
3rd Battery. 3. Supply Wagons.

Brigade halted 1½ hours at BORHAM. Arrived at WITHAM 3.p.m., and went into Billets for the night.

1st Battery complete at FREEBOURNE FARM.

2nd Battery and Brigade Headquarters Staff men at CINEMA HALL, Guns and horses in ROYAL ENGINEERS FIELD.

3rd Battery men in Billets.

2/1st SOUTH MIDLAND (GLOUCESTERSHIRE) BRIGADE, R.F.A.

WAR DIARY

Appendix No. 3.

SUMMARY OF DIVISIONAL TACTICAL EXERCISE

which took place on October 29th, 1915

MOUNTNESSING — HUTTON — SHENFIELD

Orders sent out.	Orders received
Artillery Order No.1. Disposition of Infantry Disposition of Artillery:- Left (3rd) Battery position under cover of Point 256 Centre (2nd) Battery position at first "M" in MOUNTNESSING HALL Right (1st) Battery position south of "H" in MOUNTNESSING HALL Ammunition Column (Imaginary) at "D" in SHENFIELD Starting Point. Junction RAILWAY ROAD-MAIN ROAD, INGATESTONE Starting time 8.30a.m. Battery Commanders to report results of reconnaissance at Troops rendezvous at 9.30 a.m. Brigade Headquarters at FORKED ROAD W of first "R" in RIVER WID **Artillery Order No.2.** Disposition of Infantry Field Ambulance at HUTTON PLACE **Artillery Order No.3.** Infantry withdraws 1st Battery to withdraw to position S of road running W of HUTTON HALL 11.20 a.m. Reports to Shenfield. **Artillery Order No.4.** Infantry withdraws. 2nd Battery to withdraw to position south Road South of place in HUTTON PLACE covering from "P" in HUTTON to Main RAILWAY line Sent at 11.20 a.m.	Operation Order No.30 from Col Sir John Barnsley, V.D. commanding 183rd Infantry Bde. giving positions to be occupied by Infantry and also giving vague idea of the scheme. A hostile force is advancing South from CHELMSFORD. The 61st (South Midland) is holding a defensive position north of BRENTWOOD. Operations received from Lt.Col A.R.Burrowes, General Staff 61st (S.M.) Div, giving General Idea, Special Idea, and Instructions. Register of Targets from 3rd Battery giving positions of Battery and range of Guns. 10.15a.m. Battery position received from 2nd Battery. Thick fog reported. 10.15 a.m. Battery position received from 1st Battery. Fog clearing. 10.55 a.m. Position of Wagon Line received from Ammunition Column. 11.40 a.m. New Battery position received from 1st Battery. 1.20 p.m. New Battery position received from 3rd Battery. 1.25 p.m. New Battery position received from 2nd Battery. 1.45 p.m.

Orders sent out.	Orders received

Artillery Order No.5.

Infantry withdraws 3rd Battery to support one Battalion of Infantry covering retirement of Infantry Brigade and then retire to position by first "E" in GREAT EASTERN covering from "S" in WYNBARNS to RAILWAY Line

Sent at 11.30 a.m.

Artillery Order No.6.

INTENTION to draw the enemy, after which the G.OC. Division intends to counter attack from our left flank.

Disposition of Infantry 2/3rd Field Ambulance at MIDDLETON HALL.

Army Form C. 2118.

WAR DIARY
or
INTELLIGENCE SUMMARY.

(Erase heading not required.)

Instructions regarding War Diaries and Intelligence Summaries are contained in F. S. Regs., Part II. and the Staff Manual respectively. Title pages will be prepared in manuscript.

Place	Date	Hour	Summary of Events and Information	Remarks and references to Appendices
INGATESTONE	1915 Nov 1st	—	Individual Training commenced. 2/Lt.Richards granted sick leave from 31/10/15.	
	2nd		Full complement of Stretcher Bearers (2 per unit) commenced training.	
	4th 5th 6th		Authority received to put Horses into billets. Tactical Scheme under Col.Ludlow Tactical Scheme under Sir John Barnsley, V.D. Lt.Col.Metford, V.D. acting C.R.A. 18 Remounts arrived	Appendix 1 " 2
	7th		Lt.Col.Metford V.D. relinquishes acting C.R.A. Major R.L.Austin and MAJOR E.J.Dunscombe attends 14 days course at Shoeburyness. 2/Lt.S.L.Dickenson attends a months course at Shoeburyness on 15 pr and 18 pr Q.F.	
	8th		Clipping of Horses commenced. 18 men transferred to the 3rd Line.	
	9th		Colonel Long, Inspector of Remounts, inspected Horses of this Brigade. 1st 2nd and 3rd Batteries at Ingatestone. Reported "Good" Ammunition Column at Mill Green. Report "Fair" Horse mastership of Brigade "Good". Inoculation:- 1 Officer 1st time. 25 men 1st time and 16 men 2nd time.	
	12th		Officer Commanding A.S.C. inspected 1st line Transport at Mill Green. Ammunition Column takes on duty of hauling supplies from Chelmsford	
	14th		2/Lt.Lascelles attends course on Telephones etc at Woolwich. Board of Enquiry held on 2430 Gunner Barnes 3rd Battery absent without leave.	

1577 Wt.W10791/1773 500,000 1/15 D.D.&L. A.D.S.S./Forms/C. 2118.

Army Form C. 2118.

WAR DIARY
or
INTELLIGENCE SUMMARY.
(Erase heading not required.)

Instructions regarding War Diaries and Intelligence Summaries are contained in F.S. Regs., Part II. and the Staff Manual respectively. Title pages will be prepared in manuscript.

Place	Date	Hour	Summary of Events and Information	Remarks and references to Appendices
INGATESTONE	1915 Novr			
	15th	—	Major V.A.Hillman attends as member on General Court Martial at Chelmsford	
	19th	—	Lt.Colonel F.K.S.Metford President of District Court Martial at Baddow Road Hutments, Chelmsford	
	20th	—	2/Lt.Ostler attends 14 days course at Dunstable on Cable Laying.	
	21st	—	Board of Enquiry on fatal injury to a Horse. Commanding Officer presented No.844 Gunner Wintle (Member of the band) with the Territorial Force Efficiency Medal, before the Brigade.	
	22nd	—	Major V.A.Hillman attends as member on District Court Martial at Writtle. 2/Lt.P.T.Rowe attends for instruction. Newly erected baths (By Mr.Patrick Green) taken into use by this Brigade.	
	24th	—	Mange case discovered in the Ammunition Column. Colonel Walters, A.D.V.S. 3rd Army] inspected Segregated Horses (123 Yeomanry) mange contacts. Staff Ride R.A.officers under Bde Major. BATTLESBRIDGE and WETTENDON.	
	25th	—	Board of Enquiry on fatal injury to horse No.2253. 5 Officers Cobs arrived. Lieutenant Thorne A.V.C. arrives to deal with 123 mange contact cases.	
	26th	—	All Ammunition Column Horses examined for mange by Veterinary Officer. 1st Line Transport (less Ammunition Column) inspected by Officer Commanding, A.SC. Segregated Yeomanry Horses go into Segregated Stables at Stock and Mountnessing.	
	27th	—	2/Lt.Ryder attends course efor a month at Edinburgh University.	

1577 Wt.W10791/1773 500,000 1/15 D.D.&L. A.D.S.S./Forms/C. 2118.

Army Form C. 2118.

WAR DIARY
or
INTELLIGENCE SUMMARY.
(Erase heading not required.)

Instructions regarding War Diaries and Intelligence Summaries are contained in F. S. Regs., Part II. and the Staff Manual respectively. Title pages will be prepared in manuscript.

Place	Date	Hour	Summary of Events and Information	Remarks and references to Appendices
INGATESTONE	1915 Nov. 29th	—	The following Officers attending Course of Instruction(Divisional Field Artillery Course) at INGATESTONE, under Major Austin:- 2/Lieut.C.A.Fenwick, 2/Lieut.C.Mc.Ilquham, 2/Lieut. C.H.Pearson, 2/Lieutt W.Nurse and 2/Lieut.W.H.Friend.	
	30th		All Horses of this Brigade inspected by A.D.V.S. 3rd Army. Information received Brigade to be equipped with 18 pr Equipment. 12 18pr Q.F. Ammunition Wagons and Limbers received from Ordnance, Warley, and numbered as follows:- 35356, 35357, 35358, 35360, 35362, 35364, 35365, 35366, 35367, 35368, 35369, 35370. Brigade Stghallets inspected by 3rd Army Officer. Authority given by A.D.V.S. 3rd Army for Horses to be clipped all over.	

****

Capt. P.F.A.
Adjutant.
2/1st. S. Midland (C/o 332) Bde R.F.A.

Army Form C. 2118.

WAR DIARY
or
INTELLIGENCE SUMMARY.
(Erase heading not required.)

Instructions regarding War Diaries and Intelligence Summaries are contained in F. S. Regs., Part II. and the Staff Manual respectively. Title pages will be prepared in manuscript.

Place	Date	Hour	Summary of Events and Information	Remarks and references to Appendices
INGATESTONE	1915 Novr 1st	-	Individual Training commenced. 2/Lt.Richards granted sick leave from 31/10/15.	
	2nd		Full complement of Stretcher Bearers (2 per Unit) commenced training.	
	4th		Authority received to put Horses into billets. Tactical Scheme under Col.Ludlow	Appendix
	5th 6th		Tactical Scheme under Lt.Col.Metford, V.D. acting C.R.A. Remounts arrived	"
	7th		Lt.Col.Metford V.D. relinquishes acting C.R.A. Major R.L.Austin and MAJOR E.J.Dunscombe attends 14 days course at Shoeburyness. 2/Lt.S.L.Dickenson attends a months course at Shoeburyness on 15 pr and 18 pr Q.F.	
	8th		Clipping of Horses commenced. 18 men transferred to the 3rd Line.	
	9th		Colonel Long, Inspector of Remounts, inspected Horses of this Brigade. 1st 2nd and 3rd Batteries at Ingatestone. Reported "Good" Ammunition Column at Mill Green. Report "Fair" Horse mastership of Brigade "Good". Inoculation:- 1 Officer 1st time. 25 men 1st time and 18 men 2nd time.	
	12th		Officer Commanding A.S.C. inspected 1st Line Transport at Mill Green. Ammunition Column takes on duty of hauling supplies from Chelmsford	
	14th		2/Lt.Lascelles attends course on Telephones etc at Woolwich. Board of Enquiry held on 2430 Gunner Barnes 3rd Battery absent without leave.	

1577 Wt.W10791/1773 500,000 1/15 D.D.&L. A.D.S.S./Forms/C. 2118.

Army Form C. 2118.

WAR DIARY
or
INTELLIGENCE SUMMARY.
(Erase heading not required.)

Instructions regarding War Diaries and Intelligence Summaries are contained in F. S. Regs., Part II. and the Staff Manual respectively. Title pages will be prepared in manuscript.

Place	Date	Hour	Summary of Events and Information	Remarks and references to Appendices
INGATESTONE	1915 Nov:			
	18th	—	Major V.A.Hillman attends as member on General Court Martial at Chelmsford	
	19th	—	Lt.Colonel F.K.S.Metford, President of District Court Martial at Baddow Road Hutments, Chelmsford	
	20th	—	2/Lt.Ostler attends 14 days course at Dunstable on Cable Laying.	
	21st	—	Board of Enquiry on fatal injury to a Horse. Commanding Officer presented No.844 Gunner Wintle (Member of the band) with the Territorial Force Efficiency Medal, before the Brigade.	
	22nd	—	Major V.A.Hillman attends as member on District Court Martial at Writtle. 2/Lt.P.T.Rowe attends for instruction. Newly erected baths (By Mr.Patrick Green) taken into use by this Brigade.	
	24th	—	Mange case discovered in the Ammunition Column. Colonel Walters, A.D.V.S. 3rd Army, inspected Segregated Horses (133 Yeomanry) mange contacts. Staff Ride R.A.Officers under Bde Major. BATTLESBRIDGE and ESTENDON.	
	25th	—	Board of Enquiry on fatal injury to horse No.2233. 5 Officers Cobs arrived. Lieutenant Thorne A.V.C. arrives to deal with 133 mange contact cases.	
	26th	—	All Ammunition Column Horses examined for mange by Veterinary Officer. 1st Line Transport (less Ammunition Column) inspected by Officer Commanding. A.66. Segregated Yeomanry Horses go into Segregated Stables at Stock and Mountnessing.	
	27th	—	2/Lt.Ryder attends course efor a month at Edinburgh University.	

1577 Wt.W10791/1773 500,000 1/15 D. D. & L. A.D.S.S./Forms/C. 2118.

Army Form C. 2118.

WAR DIARY
or
INTELLIGENCE SUMMARY.
(Erase heading not required.)

Instructions regarding War Diaries and Intelligence Summaries are contained in F.S. Regs., Part II. and the Staff Manual respectively. Title pages will be prepared in manuscript.

Place	Date	Hour	Summary of Events and Information	Remarks and references to Appendices
INGATESTONE	1915 Novr 29th	—	The following Officers attending Course of Instruction(Divisional Field Artillery Course) at INGATESTONE, under Major Austin:- 2/Lieut.C.A.Fenwick, 2/Lieut.C.Mc.Ilquham, 2/Lieut. C.H.Pearson, 2/Lieut: W.Nurse and 2/Lieut.W.H.Friend.	
	30th		All Horses of this Brigade inspected by A.D.V.S. 3rd Army. Information received Brigade to be equipped with 18 pr Equipment. 12 18pr Q.F. Ammunition Wagons and Limbers received from Ordnance, Marley, and numbered as follows:- 35356, 35357, 35358, 35360, 35362, 35364, 35365, 35366, 35367, 35368, 35369, 35370. Brigade Signallers inspected by 3rd Army Officer. Authority given by A.D.M.S. 3rd Army for Horses to be clipped all over.	

****

WAR DIARY

Unit. 2/1st South Midland (Gloucestershire) Brigade, R.F.A.

Division. 61st (South Midland)

Mobilization Centre Bristol

Temporary War Station.

Stations since occupied subsequent to Concentration:-

February 3rd, 1915	Northampton
April 4th, 1915	Broomfield
" 27th, 1915	Writtle
July 26th, 1915	Epping (Canvas)
September 4th, 1915	Ingatestone (Canvas)
October 25th, 1915	Ingatestone (Billets)

(a) MOBILIZATION. Steady

(b) CONCENTRATION AT WAR STATIONS (Including Railway Moves):- Concentrated

(c) ORGANIZATION FOR DEFENCE (Including Vulnerable Points):- Improving

(d) TRAINING Steadily improving

(e) DISCIPLINE Very good.

(f) ADMINISTRATION

1. Medical Services	Good
2. Veterinary Services	Good
3. Supply Services	Good
4. Transport	Good
5. Ordnance Services	Good
6. Channels of correspondence) in Routine matters)	Fair
7. Billeting and Hutting	Fairly Good
8. Range construction (Miniature)	Good
9. Supply of Remounts	Good

(g) PREPARATION OF UNITS FOR IMPERIAL SERVICE — Inoculated Officers and men nearly 100%

STATION INGATESTONE, ESSEX

DATE 3rd December, 1915

Lt. Colonel
Commanding

2/1st SOUTH MIDLAND (GLOUCESTERSHIRE) BRIGADE, R.F.A.

WAR DIARY

Appendix No.1.

SUMMARY OF TACTICAL SCHEME:-

which took place on 4th November, 1915

under COLONEL LUDLOW

EAST HANNINGFIELD — BICNACRE — DANBURY

Orders sent out	Orders received
Artillery Order No.1. Starting Point:- Road due S of first "T" in INGATESTONE Starting time 8 a.m. Messages between Headquarters, Batteries and Observing Stations will have reference to the Squared Map. For communication to Infantry Units the ½" Map will be employed. One section per Battery to be taken, full battery Staffs and as many A.C. Wagons as possible. This Brigade to form part of the MAIN BODY of the ADVANCE GUARD Brigade to be at Road Junction West of "H" in EAST HANNINGFIELD at 10.35 a.m. **Artillery Order No.2.** Information received that Infantry will attack and seize RUNSELL GREEN and two roads leading to MALDON. Batteries to concentrate fire accordingly. Ammunition Column will be at "K" in BICKNACRE Dressing Station:- EAST HANNINGFIELD Order given verbally to B.C's by Adjutant at 12.50 a.m. at road W of "S" in SALEFRITHS FARM. Positions to be taken up covering the following zones:- Right (1st) Battery Cross Roads to "R" in DANBURY Centre (2nd) Battery "R" in DANBURY to "O" in HOME CAMP Left (3rd) Battery "O" in HOME CAMP to "C" in PALACE	**Operation Orders** A raiding force (white cap bands) has been severely handled W. of CHIPPING ONGAR and is trying to regain the coast via CHELMSFORD and MALDON. The 61st (S.M) Div is advancing from WICKFORD objective DANBURY in order to cut off enemy line of retreat. Colonel W.R.Ludlow C.B., V.D. is in command of the A.G. and will issue orders at 10 a.m. Head of M.Guard at Road Junction ½ mile S. of H. in EAST HANNINGFIELD. Colonel Ludlow's orders are to attack the enemy vigourously whenever met. The 2/1st R.F.A.Bde INGATESTONE will report to Road Junction W. of H° in EAST HANNINGFIELD at 10-35 a.m. **************** Centre Battery (2nd) report at 11.40 Wagon Line in Hedge 100 yds S of second "N" in EAST HANNINGFIELD. Where is A.C.? Centre Battery report that they are ready to fire. Position of Battery at 11.50 a.m. at Bend in road N. of "S" in SALEFRITHS FARM Left (3rd) Battery report at 12 noon position of Battery N. of D of "D" in EAST HANNINGFIELD. Reference line road fork W of "D" in DANBURY. Right (1st) Battery report at 12.11 p. position of Battery N of "T" in SALEFRITHS FARM. Centre Battery report Wagon Line 100 yds N.W. of "E" in EAST HANNINGFIELD at 12.12 p.m. *** *****

Orders sent out	Orders received

Orders given verbally to B.C's by Adjutant at 12.50 p.m.

Batteries to go forward at once and take up positions in vicinity of BROCKS FARM (at DANBURY) lines laid on MALDON. Route BICKNACRE- WHITE ELM GAY BOWENS - TYNDALES - RUNSALL GREEN. The lower road is not useable as bridge is blown down.

At 1 o'clock "Cease fire" was given.

****

2/1st SOUTH MIDLAND (GLOUCESTERSHIRE) BRIGADE, R.F.A.

W A R   D I A R Y

Appendix No.1.

SUMMARY OF TACTICAL SCHEME:-

which took place on 4th November, 1915

under COLONEL LUDLOW

EAST HANNINGFIELD - BICKNACRE - DANBURY

Orders sent out	Orders received
Artillery Order No.1. Starting Point:- Road due S of first "T" in INGATESTONE Starting time 8 a.m. Messages between Headquarters, Batteries and Observing Stations will have reference to the Squared Map. For communication to Infantry Units the ½" Map will be employed. One section per Battery to be taken, full battery Staffs and as many A.C. Wagons as possible. This Brigade to form part of the MAIN BODY of the ADVANCE GUARD Brigade to be at Road Junction West of "H" in EAST HANNINGFIELD at 10.35 a.m. **Artillery Order No.2.** Information received that Infantry will attack and seize RUNSELL GREEN and two roads leading to MALDON. Batteries to concentrate fire accordingly. Ammunition Column will be at "K" in BICKNACRE Dressing Station:- EAST HANNINGFIELD **Order given verbally to B.C's by Adjutant at 11.50 a.m. at road W of "S" in SALEFRITHS FARM.** Positions to be taken up covering the following zones:- Right (1st) Battery Cross Roads to "H" in DANBURY Centre (2nd) Battery "H" in DANBURY to "O" in HOME CAMP Left (3rd) Battery "O" in HOME CAMP to "C" in PALACE	**Operation Orders** A raiding force (white cap bands) has been severely handled W. of CHIPPING ONGAR and is trying to regain the coast via CHELMSFORD and MALDON. The 61st (S.M) Div is advancing from WICKFORD objective DANBURY in order to cut off enemy line of retreat. Colonel W.R.Ludlow C.B., V.D. is in command of the A.G.and will issue orders at 10 a.m. Head of M.Guard at Road Junction ½ mile S. of H. in EAST HANNINGFIELD. Colonel Ludlow's orders are to attack the enemy vigourously whenever met. The 2/1st R.F.A.Bde INGATESTONE will report to Road Junction W. of "H" in EAST HANNINGFIELD at 10-35 a.m. **⁂⁂⁂⁂⁂⁂⁂⁂⁂⁂** Centre Battery (2nd) report at 11.40 Wagon Line in Hedge 100 yds S of second "N" in EAST HANNINGFIELD. Where is A.C.? Centre Battery report that they are ready to fire. Position of Battery at 11.50 a.m. at Bend in road N. of "S" in SALEFRITHS FARM Left (3rd) Battery report at 12 noon position of Battery S of "D" in EAST HANNINGFIELD. Reference line road fork W of "D" in DANBURY. Right (1st) Battery report at 12.11 p.m position of Battery N of "T" in SALEFRITHS FARM. Centre Battery report Wagon Line 100 yds N.W. of "E" in EAST HANNINGFIELD at 12.12 p.m. ⁂⁂⁂⁂⁂

Orders sent out	Orders received

Orders given verbally to B.C's by Adjutant at 12.50 p.m.

Batteries to go forward at once and take up positions in vicinity of BROOMS FARM (at DANBURY) lines laid on MALDON. Route BICKNACRE - WHITE ELM GAY BOWERS - TYNDALES - RUNSALL GREEN. The lower road is not usable as bridge is blown down.

At 1 o'clock "Cease fire" was given.

2/1st SOUTH MIDLAND (GLOUCESTERSHIRE) BRIGADE, R. F. A.

WAR DIARY

Appendix No. 2

SUMMARY OF TACTICAL SCHEME

which took place on NOVEMBER 5th, 1915
under Colonel Sir John Barnsley, V.D.

HUTTON — BRENTWOOD

Orders sent out	Orders received
Artillery Order No.1	**Operation Orders**
This Brigade will form part of a column composed of various Units under Command of Col.Sir.J.Barnsley, and will be at road fork N.W. of "S" in point 233 on the SHENFIELD - HUTTON - BILLERICAY road at 10 a.m.	On the night 4/5th Nov 1915 the 61st (S.M) Div billeted in the neighbourhood of BRENTWOOD. An invading force all arms was known to be in the neighbourhood of COLD NORTON. The 61st Div is under orders to move N.E. on 5th Nov. The 2/1st Bde, R.F.A. with other Units will be halted in column of route on the SHENFIELD - HUTTON - BILLERICAY road. at 10 a.m.
Starting place JUNCTION Point RAILWAY ROAD - MAIN ROAD, INGATESTONE Time 8 a.m. Haversack rations to be taken. Orders and messages between Brigade Headquarters and Batteries will have reference to the Squared Map. For communication with Infantry Units ½" Maps will be employed. One section per Battery to be taken, full Battery Staffs and as many A.C. Wagons as possible.	1st Battery reports at 11.20 a.m. position occupied E of the road by "M" in MILL HILL. Are you allotting any special zones?
Artillery Order No.2.	2nd Battery reports at 11.10 a.m. Battery position H.7@ 63. O.P.H.8 b 41. Line laid out 85 Mag.
Force of enemy all arms advancing through RETTENDON at 9.30 a.m. reported by Aeroplane. Intention to seize high ground "E" of BILLERICAY. Infantry line will be MILL HILL to "W" in NURSEY WOOD. Disposition of Infantry, Disposition of Artillery:- 1st Battery will support Right flank. 2nd Battery will support Centre 3rd " " " Left.	2nd Battery reported Wagon Line is 100 yds N of "T" in TYE COMMON 11.35 a.m.
	1st Battery reports at 11.45 a.m. Observing position H.8.d.65 Battery Position H.8.C.35
	3rd Battery reports at 11.50 a.m. Position H.3.a.06. Enemy scouts about 40 N of my position on main STOCK road.
Reports to Cross Roads S of "A" in BILLERICAY. Ammunition Column by point 166.	Ammunition Column reports at 11.55 a.m. Position G.6.c.31.
Artillery Order No.3. Message sent by Mounted Orderly to all Batteries "Open fire when enemy is observed. 11.50 a.m.	3rd Battery at 12.50 p.m. reports Observing Station H.3.c.88. Ready to open fire.

****

Orders sent out.	Orders received

Message sent by Mounted Orderly at
12.15 p.m. to Left (3rd) Battery
Where is your Observing Station?

Artillery Order No.4.

Batteries will proceed home by the following routes,

Cross roads S of "A" in BILLERICAY -through "A" in BILLERICAY.- LAWLESS through "F" in FORD - INGATESTONE STABLES.

Ammunition Column will proceed by same route.

****

CONFIDENTIAL

WAR DIARY of

2/1st SOUTH MIDLAND (Glos) BRIGADE, R. F. A.

from 1st December, 1915 to 31st December, 1915.

****

Volume 1.

CONFIDENTIAL

WAR DIARY of

2/1st SOUTH MIDLAND (GLOS) BRIGADE, R. F. A.

from 1st December, 1915 to 31st December, 1915.

==============

Volume 1.

WAR DIARY
or
INTELLIGENCE SUMMARY

(Erase heading not required.)

Army Form C. 2118

Place	Date	Hour	Summary of Events and Information	Remarks and references to Appendices
INGATESTONE	1915 Dec 1st		Captain B.C.Biggar (Capt) relinquishes Commission in the Territorial Force – November 12th, 1915. Lieutenant H.B.Logan to be temporary Captain. November 26th, 1915 Gazette:- F.L.Perowne, H.T.Roberts & F.J.Baly to be 2/Lieutenants in this Brigade. 2/Lieutenant E.S.L.Ostler transferred from 3rd Battery to Headquarter Staff.	a/µ
	2nd		40 men inoculated.	a/µ
	3rd		Colonel Rutherford A.D.V.S. O.F. Inspected Mange Contact Cases. 7 S.A.A. Limbered Wagons arrived for Ammunition Column. Numbers E.89938 to E.89944 inclusive	a/µ
	4th		2/Lieutenant G.H.Lascelles attends 18pr Gunnery Course at Shoeburyness	a/µ
	5th		Church Parade 10 a.m. 2/Lieutenant S.L.Dickenson transferred from Ammunition Column to 2nd Battery	a/µ
	6th		Inspection by Major General Brunker, Inspector R.H. & R.F.A. Unable to parade mounted owing to Mange. 3rd Batteries at Battery Gun Drill were inspected in their respective Gun Parks, Signallers, and spare men at Foot Drill. Also some horses. Model Range Board inspected. Rev.H.M.Porter appointed officiating Clergy C of E. to this Brigade whilst at Ingatestone. Inspection report:- Gunnery quite above average, Discipline Good.	a/µ
	8th		6 18pr Guns arrived from Vickers. Gun numbers 33328 to 33333 inclusive. 1200 rounds (300 cases) 18pr Q.F. Ammunition received at Ingatestone. Transported from Chelmsford by A.S.C.	a/µ
	9th		2/Leieut H.T.Roberts posted to 1st Battery, 2/Lieut.F.J.Baly to 3rd Battery and 2/Lieut. F.L.Perowne to Ammunition Column. 24 Ammunition Wagons and Limbers and 12 Gun Limbers 18 pr Q.F. fetched from Shenfield Station and numbered as follows:- 24 Ammunition Wagons and Limbers C.32265 to C.32288 inclusive. Gun Limbers C.32072, C.32113, C.32115, C.39124, C.39202 to C.39207 C.39209 to C.39211 inclusive.	a/µ
	10th		1 18pr Q.F. Gun arrived at Ingatestone from Vickers) Numbers C.33334 to C.33339 inclusive.	a/µ
	11th		5 18pr Q.F. Guns arrived at Ingatestone from Vickers) (This completes the Brigades Establishment of Guns & Wagons 18pr Q.F)	a/µ

Army Form C. 2118

WAR DIARY
or
INTELLIGENCE SUMMARY

(Erase heading not required.)

Instructions regarding War Diaries and Intelligence [Summ]aries are contained in F. S. Regs., Part II. and the Staff Manual respectively. Title Pages will be prepared in manuscript.

Place	Date	Hour	Summary of Events and Information	Remarks and references to Appendices
INGATESTONE	1915 Decr 11th		Lt.Col F.K.S.Metford on leave (11th to 13th Decr) Major E.J.Dunscombe commanding Brigade.	M/M
	12th	10a.m	Church Parade	M/M
	13th		Lieut.H.V.Cope transfers to 3rd Line. Major E.J.Dunscombe Member of District Court Martial at Officers Mess 2/1st S.M.R.G.A. Chelmsford. Captain G.S.James attends for instruction.	M/M
	13-18th		Company Sergt Major Ridgewell, Army Gymnastic Staff instructs 3 N.C.O's per Unit in Physical Exercises.	M/M
	13th		Guns and Wagons allotted to Batteries as per Appendice.	Appendix "A" M/M
	17th		Lt.Col.F.K.S.Metford President of District Court Martial at Officers Mess 2/4th S.M. (H) Bde,R.F.A Major V.A.Hillman attends for as Member and 2/Lieut.P.T.Rowe attends for Instruction.	M/M
	17-20th		Lt.Col.F.K.S.Metford acting C.R.A.	M/M
	20th	10a.m.	Church Parade. 2nd Battery moves to Margaretting (Billets) Old system of fetching supplies from Chelmsford superceded by Officer i/c Supplies 183rd Inf Brigade bringing supplies to Ingatestone from Brentwood.	M/M
	22nd		5 days leave with free Warrant commenced. Princess Mary's Gift Boxes received for those serving on the 24th December, 1914	M/M
	25th	10 a.m	Church Parade	M/M
	28th		Special instruction 18 pr Gun Drill commences 9.15 a.m. to 10.15 a.m. daily for Officers (Under B) and (Unles otherwise specified, drill is carried out daily by each Battery	M/M

Army Form C. 2118

Instructions regarding War Diaries and Intelligence Summaries are contained in F.S. Regs, Part II. and the Staff Manual respectively. Title Pages will be prepared in manuscript.

WAR INTELLIGENCE DIARY
(Erase heading not required.)

Place	Date	Hour	Summary of Events and Information	Remarks and references to Appendices
INGATESTONE	1915 Dec 1st		Captain B.C.Biggar relinquishes Commission in the Territorial Force - November 12th, 1915. Lieutenant H.B.Logan to be temporary Captain. November 26th, 1915 Gazette:- F.L.Perowne, H.T.Roberts & F.J.Baly to be 2/Lieutenants in this Brigade. 2 Lieutenant E.S.L.Ostler transferred from 3rd Battery to Headquarter Staff.	
	2nd		40 men inoculated.	
	3rd		Colonel Rutherford A.D.V.S. C.F. inspected Mange Contact Cases. 7 S.A.A. Limbered Wagons arrived for Ammunition Column. Numbers E.89938 to E.89944 inclusive	
	4th		2/Lieutenant G.H.Lascelles attends 18pr Gunnery Course at Shoeburyness	
	5th		Church Parade 10 a.m. 2/Lieutenant S.L.Dickenson transferred from Ammunition Column to 2nd Battery	
	6th		Inspection by Major General Brunker, Inspector R.H. & R.F.A. Unable to parade mounted owing to Mange. 3rd Batteries at Battery Gun Drill were inspected in their respective Gun Parks Signallers and spare men at Foot Drill. Also some horses. Model Range Board inspected. Rev. H.M.Porter appointed officiating Clergy C of E, to this Brigade whilst at Ingatestone. Inspection report:- Gunnery quite above average. Discipline Good. 6 18pr Guns arrived from Vickers. Gun numbers 33328 to 33333 inclusive. 1200 rounds (300 cases) 18pr Q.F. Ammunition received at Ingatestone. Transported from Chelsford by A.S.C.	
	8th			
	9th		2/Lieut H.T.Roberts posted to 1st Battery, 2/Lieut.F.J.Baly to 3rd Battery and 2/Lieut. F.L.Perowne to Ammunition Column. 24 Ammunition Wagons and Limbers and 12 Gun Limbers 18 pr Q.F. fetched from Sherfield Station and numbered as follows:- 24 Ammunition Wagons and Limbers C.32265 to C.32288 inclusive. Gun Limbers C.32072, C.32115, C.59124, C.59202 to C.59207 C.59209 to C.59211 inclusive.	
	10th		1 18pr Q.F. Gun arrived at Ingatestone from Vickers } Numbers C.33334 to C.33339 inclusive. 5 18pr Q.F. Guns arrived at Ingatestone from Vickers }	
	11th		(This completes the Brigades Establishment of Guns & Wagons 18pr Q.F.)	

Army Form C. 2118

WAR DIARY
or
INTELLIGENCE SUMMARY

(Erase heading not required.)

Instructions regarding War Diaries and Intelligence Summaries are contained in F.S. Regs., Part II. and the Staff Manual respectively. Title Pages will be prepared in manuscript.

Place	Date	Hour	Summary of Events and Information	Remarks and references to Appendices
INGATESTONE	1915 Decr 11th		Lt.Col F.K.S.Metford on leave (11th to 13th Decr) Major E.J.Dunscombe commanding Brigade.	
	12th	10a.m	Church Parade	
	13th		Lieut.H.V.Cope transfers to 3rd Line. Major E.J.Dunscombe Member of District Court Martial at Officers Mess 2/1st S.M.R.G.A. Chelmsford. Captain G.S.James attends for instruction. Company Sergt Major Ridgewell, Army Gymnastic Staff instructs 3 N.C.O's per Unit in Physical Exercises.	Appendix "A"
	13-18th			
	15th		Guns and Wagons allotted to Batteries as per Appendice.	
	17th		Lt.Col.F.K.S.Metford President of District Court Martial at Officers Mess 2/4th S.M. (B) Bde,RFA Major V.A.Hillman attends for as Member and 2/Lieut.P.T.Rowe attends for Instruction.	
	17-20th		Lt.Col.F.K.S.Metford acting C.R.A.	
	20th	10a.m.	Church Parade 2nd Battery moves to Margaretting (Billets) Old system of fetching supplies from Chelmsford superceded by Officer i/c Supplies 183rd Inf Brigade bringing supplies to Ingatestone from Brentwood.	
	22nd		5 days leave with free Warrant commenced. Princess Mary's Gift Boxes received for those serving on the 24th December, 1914	
	25th	10 a.m	Church Parade	
	28th		Special Instruction 18 pr Gun Drill commences 9.15 a.m. to 10.15 a.m. daily for Officers (Unless otherwise specified, drill is carried out daily by each Battery)	

Appendix "A"

ALLOTMENT TO BATTERIES OF 18 pr GUNS AND WAGONS

GUNS AND LIMBERS

1st Battery		2nd Battery		3rd Battery	
Guns	Limbers	Guns	Limbers	Guns	Limbers
C.33328	C.32072	C.33332	C.39203	C.33336	C.39207
C.33329	C.32113	C.33333	C.39204	C.33337	C.39209
C.33330	C.39124	C.33334	C.39205	C.33338	C.39210
C.33331	C.39202	C.33335	C.39206	C.33339	C.39211

AMMUNITION WAGONS AND LIMBERS

1st Battery	2nd Battery	3rd Battery	Ammn Column
C.32265	C.32273	C.32281	C.35356
C.32266	C.32274	C.32282	C.35357
C.32267	C.32275	C.32283	C.35358
C.32268	C.32276	C.32284	C.35360
C.32269	C.32277	C.32285	C.35362
C.32270	C.32278	C.32286	C.35364
C.32271	C.32279	C.32287	C.35365
C.32272	C.32280	C.32288	C.35366
~~C.32275~~			C.35367
			C.35368
			C.35369
			C.35370
			S.A.A.
			E.89938
			E.89939
			E.89940
			E.89941
			E.89942
			E.89943
			E.89944

Appendix "A"

ALLOTMENT TO BATTERIES OF 18 pr GUNS AND WAGONS

GUNS AND LIMBERS

1st Battery		2nd Battery		3rd Battery	
Guns	Limbers	Guns	Limbers	Guns	Limbers
C.33328	C.39072	C.33332	C.39203	C.33336	C.39207
C.33329	C.38113	C.33333	C.39204	C.33337	C.39209
C.33330	C.39184	C.33334	C.39205	C.33338	C.39210
C.33331	C.39202	C.33335	C.39206	C.33339	C.39211

AMMUNITION WAGONS AND LIMBERS

1st Battery	2nd Battery	3rd Battery	Amn Column
C.32265	C.32273	C.32281	C.35356
C.32266	C.32274	C.32282	C.35357
C.32267	C.32275	C.32283	C.35358
C.32268	C.32276	C.32284	C.35360
C.32269	C.32277	C.32285	C.35362
C.32270	C.32278	C.32286	C.35364
C.32271	C.32279	C.32287	C.35365
C.32272	C.32280	C.32288	C.35366
			C.35367
			C.35368
			C.35369
			C.35370
			S.A.A.
			E.89938
			E.89939
			E.89940
			E.89941
			E.89942
			E.89943
			E.89944

CONFIDENTIAL

WAR DIARY of

2/1st SOUTH MIDLAND (Glos) BRIGADE, R. F. A.

from 1st January, 1916 to 31st January, 1916

****

Volume 2.

WAR DIARY
or
INTELLIGENCE SUMMARY
(Erase heading not required.)

Army Form C. 2118

Reference 2 " O.S. Sheet 20

Place	Date	Hour	Summary of Events and Information	Remarks and references to Appendices
INGATESTONE ESSEX 1916	Jany 1st		2/Lieut.S.L.Dickenson transferred from 2nd to 1st Battery 2/Lieut.M.J.Richards transferred from 1st Battery to Ammunition Column. 2/Lieut.W.J.Rowden granted 14 days Sick Leave. Capt.H.B.Logan relinquishes Commission in T.F.	On
	2nd	10a.m.	Church Parade	On
	3rd		Lt.Col.F.K.S.Metford, V.D. proceeded overseas & attached to Gen HdQrs for course of Instruction for 5 days. Major R.L.Austin assumes Command of Brigade.	On
	4th		Major Austin President of District Court Martial held at OFFICERS MESS, 2/4th S.M. (H) Bde, RFA WRITTLE. Lieut.Rowden, B.A. attended for Instruction. 5 men attended Medical Board at OAKLANDS HOSPITAL, CHELMSFORD. All passed for Home Service only.	On
	5th		Sergt.Noakes, 16th Lancers Instructor in Equitation arrived for duty. Instructed Officers & N.C.O's in Equitation from 5th to 18th January.	On
	7th		Lt.Col.F.K.S.Metford, V.D. returns from overseas and assumes Command of Brigade. 6 G.S.Wagons arrived and allotted 2 to each Battery.	On
	9th	10a.m.	Church Parade	On
	10th		6 G.S.Wagons arrived and allotted to Ammn Column. Inoculation of men took place. Lecture by Lt.Col Metford on his experiencies at the front.	On
	11th		2/Lieut.Lascelles attached HeadQr Staff as Temporary Orderly Officer. 2/Lieut.C.McIlquham transferred from 3rd to 2nd Battery. 2/Lieut.Lascelles, G.J.H. transferred from 2nd Battery to Ammunition Column. 2/Lieut.B.H.Ryder transferred 1st Battery to Ammn Col.	On

WAR DIARY or INTELLIGENCE SUMMARY

(Erase heading not required.)

Army Form C. 2118

Instructions regarding War Diaries and Intelligence Summaries are contained in F.S. Regs., Part II. and the Staff Manual respectively. Title Pages will be prepared in manuscript.

Reference b "O.S. Sheet 30"

Place	Date	Hour	Summary of Events and Information	Remarks and references to Appendices
INGATESTONE ESSEX	1916 Jany 12th		Major E.J.Dunscombe member of District Court Martial held at VILLAGE HALL, WRITTLE. Captain G.P.Lindrea attended for instruction. 1 G.S.Wagon arrived and allotted to Headquarter Staff.	On.
	13th		4 15prB.L.C. Guns taken over from 60th Division. 2/Lieut.Perowne attached to 2nd Battery for duty.	On.
	14th		Brigade took part in Tactical Scheme under Sir J.Barnsley, V.D. at BILLERICAY. 23 Officers 321 N.C.O's & men, 10 18pr Guns, 36 Wagons and 301 Horses turned out and took part. 5 men transferred to Home Service Details, COLCHESTER 1 A.V.C. Sergt attached for Veterinary duty.	Appendix No.1. On.
	15th		Capt A.G.Noble attached for Course of instruction overseas with B.E.Force. 2/Lieut.W.Nurse appointed a/Adjutant.	On.
	16th	10a.m	Church Parade 2/Lieut.J.C.Fielding attends 10 days Course of Instruction at ORDNANCE COLLEGE, WOOLWICH. 2/Lieut.C.H.Pearson attends 4 weeks Gunnery Course at SHOEBURYNESS.	On. On.
	17th		7 G.S. Wagons arrived and allotted to Ammunition Column.	On.
	19th		Lieut.S.A.Rowden gazetted temporary Captain.	On.
	21st		All Horses inspected by Divisional Remount Officer. Lt.Col.F.K.S.Metford, V.D. President of District Court Martial held at OFFICERS MESS, GT.BADDOW. Major Hillman Member of same, and Capt.G.S.James attended for instruction.	On.
	23rd	10a.M	Church Parade	On.
	24th		Board of Enquiry held to enquire into accident to Transport Wagon and damage done. President Capt.E.S.Harris, Members Lieut.W.N.Unwin and 2/Lieut.S.L.Dickenson. 2/Lieut.E.S.L.Ostler attends 6 weeks Signalling Course at 3rd ARMY SIGNALLING SCHOOL, DUNMOW. Board held for condemning unserviceable Clothing. Major Hillman, President. Members, 2/Lieut. C.McIlquham and 2/Lieut.Friend.	On.

Army Form C. 2118

WAR DIARY
or
INTELLIGENCE SUMMARY
(Erase heading not required)

Instructions regarding War Diaries and Intelligence Summaries are contained in F. S. Regs., Part II. and the Staff Manual respectively. Title Pages will be prepared in manuscript.

Reference 2 A.L. Sheet 30

Place	Date	Hour	Summary of Events and Information	Remarks and references to Appendices
INGATESTONE ESSEX	1916 Jany 24th		35 Recruits arrived and posted 10 to 1st Battery, 20 to 2nd Battery and 5 to 3rd Battery. 2/Lieut.R.H.Maddock reported for duty.	On
	25th		Court of Enquiry held into illegal absence of 2108 Dr.Smith. President Capt.B.A.Rowden, Members 2/Lieut.P.T.Rowe and 2/Lieut.M.J.Richards. 2/Lieut.Perowne attached to 1st Battery for duty.	On
	27th		Brigade took part in Tactical Exercise under Sir.J.Barnsley, V.D. SHENFIELD and BRENTWOOD. 25 Officers, 320 N.C.O's and men, 12 Guns 18pr, 35 Wagons and 294 Horses turned out and took part.	Appendix No.2 On
	28th		Medical Board held at INGATESTONE on all Officers as to their fitness for overseas. 2/Lieut.S.L.Dickenson attends Course on Telephones and Cable Laying at DUNSTABLE. 40 G.S.Wagons, 1 Sergt, 1 Corpl, 4 Gunners and 8 Drivers proceeded to SOUTHMINSTER for duty with the 59th (North Midland) Division.	On
	30th	10am	Church Parade.	On
	31st		Sergt.Wood S.H. attends 4 weeks Gunnery Course 18pr Q.F. at LARKHILL.	On

(Unless otherwise specified, drill is carried out by each Battery daily)

****

Lt. Colonel,
Commanding
2/1st S. Midland (Gloster) Bde. R.F.A.

2/1st SOUTH MIDLAND (GLOUCESTERSHIRE) BRIGADE, R. F. A.

WAR DIARY.

Appendix No.1.

SUMMARY OF TACTICAL SCHEME which took place

on JANUARY 14th, 1916.

BILLERICAY.

Orders Sent out.	Reference ½" O.S.Sheet 30	Orders received.
Artillery Order No.1. Batteries & column will parade ready to move off at 9.15 a.m. Head of column at BRIDGE over STREAM South of 1st B in INGATESTONE. Troops Rendezvous:- ROAD JUNCTION SHENFIELD - BILLERICAY Road East of Point 166 at 10.45 a.m. Brigade will proceed via LAWNESS. Dress - Marching Order Haversack Rations to be taken. **Artillery Order No.2.** G.O.C. intends to take up defensive position. Infantry line across MILL HILL. Artillery Lines:- 1st Battery:- SYM to WHITES FARM. 2nd Battery:- WHITES FARM TO WHITES BRIDGE 3rd Battery:- WHITES FARM TO CRAYS HILL. Dressing Station: BILLERICAY. Reports to RISING SUN, BILLERICAY. Message T.V.1. to all Batteries:- Position of Ammn Column is H.7.b.3.6. on squared map. Message T.V.2 to Ammn Column Your position will be H.7.b.3-6. I have advised Batteries. Message T.V.3. to Ammn Column Water & feed. Fall in and await orders at 2 p.m. Message T.V.4. to all Batteries:- Brigade to fall in on the road facing North Head of COLUMN RISING Sun 2 p.m. Water & Feed. ***		Operation Order No.37 from Col.Sir J.Barnsley, V.D. Commanding 183rd Inf Bde. On night of 13/14th Jany, 1916 the 61st Div billeted in neighbourhood of BRENTWOOD. Invading Force all arms landed at SOUTHEND and moving on BILLERICAY with apparent intention of cutting LONDON main Railway Line. A column composed of 2/1st S.M.Bde R.F.A. 183rd Inf Bde, 2/3rd Fd Amb, will be at BILLERICAY at 11a.m. and take up defensive position along main line of Railway. Column rendezvous ROAD JUNCTION SHENFIELD -BILLERICAY ROAD E of point 166 at 10.45 a.m. All messages to be send to Headquarters at head of Column Message from 1st battery:- Position H.14 a. 8.10. F.O.O. H.14.a.10.3. 12 noon. Message from 2nd Battery:- Position H.8.d.2.3. O.P. H.14.b.8.9. Wagon Line 50 yds of T in TYE COMMON. 12.5 p.m. Message from 3rd Battery:- Position H.8.d.5.4. O.S. H.14.b.8.9. ************

2/1st SOUTH MIDLAND (GLOUCESTERSHIRE) BRIGADE, R.F.A.

WAR DIARY.

Appendix No.2.

SUMMARY OF TACTICAL SCHEME which took place on JANUARY 27th, 1916

SHENFIELD — BRENTWOOD

Reference 1" O.S. Sheet 108.

Orders sent out.	Orders received.
Artillery Order No.1. Batteries and Column will parade ready to move off at 9.a.m. Starting Point ROAD JUNCTION W of first "I" in INGATESTONE STATION. Troops Rendezvous:- ROAD JUNCTION of the SHENFIELD - BILLERICAY road with the main CHELMSFORD- LONDON road by the second "N" in INN at 10 a.m. Dress:- Marching Order Haversack rations to be taken. **Artillery Order No.2.** G.O.C. intends to attack enemy's position S.W. of THORNDON PARK along contour line between two lakes marked 200. Infantry Line THORNDON HALL to boundary THORNDON PARK. Artillery Lines:- Supporting Infantry Line. Dressing Station:- FARM at Point 266. Hospital:- THORNDON HALL Reports to Lodge W entrance THORNDON PARK. Message T.V.1 to all Batteries:- Asking for positions of Batteries. Message T.V.2. to Ammn Column. You will take up position in a field W. of INGRAVE GREEN. Report exact position and time occupied. Message T.V.3. to all Batteries. Operations ceased. Cease firing. Water and feed. Rendezvous FORK ROADS W. of THORNDON PARK. Message T.V.4. to M.O. & staff. Same as No.3.	Operation Order No.38 from Col.Sir J.Barnsley, V.D. Commanding 183rd Inf Bde, On night Jan 26/27th an invading Force of all arms has reached EAST HORNDON and has taken up entrenched position S.E. of THORNDON PARK. A force composed of 2/1st R.F.A. Bde, 183rd Inf Bde and 2/3rd Field Amb, is ordered to attack the enemy and either destroy or capture him. Place of assembly will be at SHENFIELD 10 a.m. at JUNCTION of SHENFIELD- BILLERICAY ROAD with CHELMSFORD - LONDON ROAD by second N in INN All messages to Headquarters at Head of Column. Message from 1st Battery Position 1/8 mile N.E. of Y in WARLEY BARRACKS. Message from 2nd Battery. Position on squared Map G.26. A.98 to B.28. O.S. G.26.B.9.1. Message from 3rd Battery Position G.20 d.5.8. Line of fire laid on enemy's position G.29.d.1.6. Range 1,600. Message from Ammn Column. Position N of HARTS HOUSE at S of point 308. Time occupied 12.30 p.m. *********

CONFIDENTIAL

WAR DIARY of

2/1st SOUTH MIDLAND (Glos) BRIGADE, R. F. A.

from 1st January, 1916 to 31st January, 1916

****

Volume 2.

Army Form C. 2118

WAR DIARY
or
INTELLIGENCE SUMMARY

(Erase heading not required.)

Instructions regarding War Diaries and Intelligence Summaries are contained in F. S. Regs., Part II. and the Staff Manual respectively. Title Pages will be prepared in manuscript.

Place	Date	Hour	Summary of Events and Information	Remarks and references to Appendices
INGATESTONE ESSEX	Jany 1916 1st		2/Lieut.E.L.Dickenson transferred from 2nd to 1st Battery. 2/Lieut.E.J.Richards transferred from 1st Battery to Ammunition Column. 2/Lieut.W.J.Rowden granted 14 days Sick Leave. Capt.H.B.Logan relinquishes Commission in T.F.	
	2nd	10a.m.	Church Parade	
	3rd		Lt.Col.F.K.B.Metford, V.D. proceeded overseas & attached to Gen HdQrs for course of Instruction for 6 days. Major R.L.Austin assumes Command of Brigade.	
	4th		Major Austin President of District Court Martial held at Officers Mess, 2/4th S.M. (H) Bde,R.A Writtle. Lieut.Rowden, S.A. attended for Instruction. 8 Men attended Medical Board at Oaklands Hospital, Chelmsford. All passed for Home Service only.	
	5th		Sergt.Noakes, 18th Lancers Instructor in Equitation arrived for duty. Instructed Officers & N.C.O:s in Equitation from 5th to 13th January.	
	7th		Lt.Col.F.K.S.Metford, V.D. returns from overseas and assumes Command of Brigade. 6 G.S.Wagons arrived and allotted 2 to each Battery.	
	9th	10a.m.	Church Parade	
	10th		6 G.S.Wagons arrived and allotted to Ammn Column. Inoculation of men took place. Lecture by Lt.Col Metford on his experiencies at the front.	
	11th		2/Lieut.Lascelles attached HeadQr Staff as Temporary Orderly Officer. 2/Lieut.C.McIlquham transferred from 3rd to 2nd Battery. 2/Lieut.Lascelles, G.J.H. transferred from 2nd Battery to Ammunition Column. 2/Lieut.R.H.Ryder transferred 1st Battery to Ammn Col.	

Army Form C. 2118

WAR DIARY
or
INTELLIGENCE SUMMARY
(Erase heading not required.)

Instructions regarding War Diaries and Intelligence Summaries are contained in F. S. Regs., Part II. and the Staff Manual respectively. Title Pages will be prepared in manuscript.

Place	Date	Hour	Summary of Events and Information	Remarks and references to Appendices
INGATESTONE ESSEX	1916 Jany 12th		Major E.J.Duncombe member of District Court Martial held at Village Hall, Writtle. Captain G.P.Lindren attended for instruction. 1 G.S.Wagon arrived and allotted to Headquarter Staff.	
	13th		4.15prB.L.C. Guns taken over from 80th Division. 2/Lieut.Perowne attached to 2nd Battery for duty.	
	14th		Brigade took part in Tactical Scheme under Sir J.Barnsley, V.D. at BILLERICAY. 23 Officers 321 N.C.O's & men, 10 18pr Guns, 38 Wagons and 301 Horses turned out and took part. 5 men transferred to Home Service Details, Colchester 1 A.V.C. Sergt attached for Veterinary duty.	Appendix No.1.
	15th		Capt A.C.Noble attached for Course of Instruction overseas with B.E.Force. 2/Lieut.W.Nurse appointed a/Adjutant.	
	16th	10a.m	Church Parade 2/Lieut.J.C.Fielding attends 10 days Course of Instruction at Ordnance College, Woolwich. 2/Lieut.C.RPearson attends 4 weeks Gunnery Course at Shoeburyness.	
	17th		7 G.S.Wagons arrived and allotted to Ammunition Column.	
	19th		Lieut.S.A.Rosden Gazetted temporary Captain.	
	21st		All Horses inspected by Divisional Remount Officer. Lt.Col.F.K.E.Ketford, V.D. President of District Court Martial held at Officers Mess, Gt.Baddow. Major Hillman Member of same, and Capt.G.S.James attended for instruction.	
	23rd	10a.M	Church Parade	
	24th		Board of Enquiry held to enquire into accident to Transport Wagon and damage done. President Capt.E.S.Harris, Members Lieut.W.N.Unwin and 2/Lieut.S.L.Dickerson. 2/Lieut.E.S.L.Ostler attends 6 weeks Signalling Course at 3rd Army Signalling School, Dunmow. Board held for condemning unserviceable Clothing. Major Hillman, President, Members, 2/Lieut. C.McIlquham and 2/Lieut.Friend.	

Army Form C. 2118

WAR DIARY
or
INTELLIGENCE SUMMARY

(Erase heading not required.)

Instructions regarding War Diaries and Intelligence Summaries are contained in F. S. Regs., Part II. and the Staff Manual respectively. Title Pages will be prepared in manuscript.

Place	Date	Hour	Summary of Events and Information	Remarks and references to Appendices
INGATESTONE ESSEX	1916 Jany 24th		35 Recruits arrived and posted 10 to 1st Battery, 20 to 2nd Battery and 5 to 3rd Battery. 2/Lieut.R.H.Maddock reported for duty.	
	25th		Court of Enquiry held into illegal absence of 2105 Dr.Smith. President Capt.J.A.Rowden.Members 2/Lieut.P.T.Howe and 2/Lieut.M.J.Richards. 2/Lieut.Percowne attached to 1st Battery for duty.	
	27th		Brigade took part in Tactical Exercise under Sir.J.Barnsley, V.D. SHENFIELD and BRENTWOOD. 23 Officers, 520 N.C.O's and men, 12 Guns 18pr, 28 Wagons and 294 Horses turned out and took part.	Appendix No.2
	28th		Medical Board held at Ingatestone on all Officers as to their fitness for overseas. 2/Lieut.S.L.Dickenson attends Course on Telephones and Cable Laying at Dunstable. 4# G.S.Wagons, 1 Sergt, 1 Corpl, 4 Gunners and 8 Drivers proceeded to Southminster for duty with the 59th (North Midland) Division.	
	30th	10am	Church Parade.	
	31st		Sergt.Wood S.H. attends 4 weeks Gunnery Course 18pr Q.F. at Larkhill.	

****

2/1st SOUTH MIDLAND (GLOUCESTERSHIRE) BRIGADE, R. F. A.

W A R   D I A R Y.

Appendix No.1.

SUMMARY OF TACTICAL SCHEME which took place

on JANUARY 14th, 1916.

BILLERICAY.

Orders sent out. Ref 1/2" O.S. Sheet 30	Orders received.
Artillery Order No.1. Batteries & column will parade ready to move off at 9.15 a.m. Head of column at Bridge over Stream South of 1st B in INGATESTONE. Troops Rendezvous:- Road Junction SHENFIELD - BILLERICAY Road East of Point 166 at 10.45 a.m. Brigade will proceed via LAWNESS. Dress - Marching Order Haversack Rations to be taken. **Artillery Order No.2.** G.O.C. intends to take up defensive position. Infantry line across Mill Hill. Artillery Lines:- 1st Battery:- SYM to WHITES FARM. 2nd Battery:- WHITES FARM TO WHITES BRIDGE 3rd Battery:- WHITES FARM TO CRAYS HILL. Dressing Station: BILLERICAY. Reports to Rising Sun, Billericay. Message T.V.1. to all Batteries:- Position of Ammn Column is H.7.b.3.6. on squared map. Message T.V.2 to Ammn Column Your position will be H.7.b.3-6. I have advised Batteries. Message T.V.3. to Ammn Column Water & feed. Fall in and await orders at 2 p.m. Message T.V. 4. to all Batteries:- Brigade to fall in on the road facing North Head of Column Rising Sun 2 p.m. Water & Feed.	Operation Order No.57 from Col.Sir J.Barnsley, V.D. Commanding 183rd Inf Bde. On night of 13/14th Jany, 1916 the 61st Div billeted in neighbourhood of BRENTWOOD. Invading Force all arms landed at SOUTHEND and moving on BILLERICAY with apparent intention of cutting London main Railway Line. A column composed of 2/1st S.M.Bde R.F.A. 183rd Inf Bde, 2/3rd Fd Amb, will be at BILLERICAY at 11a.m. and take up defensive position along main line of Railway. Column rendezvous road Junction SHENFIELD -BILLERICAY road E of point 166 at 10.45 a.m. All messages to be send to Headquarters at head of Column Message from 1st battery:- Position H.14 a. 8.10. F.O.O. H.14.a.10.3. 12 noon. Message from 2nd Battery:- Position H.8.d.2.3. O.P. H.14.b.8.9. Wagon Line 50 yds of T in TYE COMMON. 12.5 p.m. Message from 3rd Battery:- Position H.8.d.5.4. O.S. H.14.b.8.9.

2/1st SOUTH MIDLAND (GLOUCESTERSHIRE) BRIGADE, R.F.A.

WAR DIARY.

Appendix No.2.

SUMMARY OF TACTICAL SCHEME which took place

on JANUARY 27th, 1916

SHENFIELD — BRENTWOOD

Orders sent out. Ref 1" Sheet of 104	Orders received.
Artillery Order No.1. Batteries and Column will parade ready to move off at 9.a.m. Starting Point Road Junction W of first "I" in INGATESTONE STATION. Troops Rendezvous:- Road Junction of the SHENFIELD – BILLERICAY road with the main CHELMSFORD– LONDON road by the second "N" in INN at 10 a.m. Dress:- Marching Order Haversack rations to be taken. **Artillery Order No.2.** G.O.C. intends to attack enemy's position S.W. of THORNDON PARK along contour line between two lakes marked 200. Infantry Line THORNDON HALL to boundary THORNDON PARK. Artillery Lines:- Supporting Infantry Line. Dressing Station:- Farm at Point 266. Hospital:- THORNDON HALL Reports to Lodge W entrance THORNDON PARK. Message T.V.1 to all Batteries:- Asking for positions of Batteries. Message T.V.2.to Ammn Column. You will take up position in a field W. of INGRAVE GREEN. Report exact position and time occupied. Message T.V.3. to all Batteries. Operations ceased. Cease firing. Water and feed. Rendezvous fork roads W. of THORNDON PARK. Message T.V.4. to M.O. & staff. Same as No.3.	Operation Order No.38 from Col.Sir J.Barnsley, V.D. Commanding 183rd Inf Bde, On night Jan 26/27th an invading Force of all arms has reached EAST HORNDON and has taken up entrenched position S.E. of THORNDON PARK. A force composed of 2/1st R.F.A. Bde, 183rd Inf Bde and 2/3rd Field Amb, is ordered to attack the enemy and either destroy or capture him. Place of assembly will be at SHENFIELD 10 a.m. at Junction of SHENFIELD– BILLERICAY road with CHELMSFORD – LONDON road by second N in INN All messages to Headquarters at head of Column. Message from 1st Battery Position 1/8 mile N.E. of Y In WARLEY BARRACKS. Message from 2nd Battery. Position on squared Map G.26. A.9.3 to R.28. O.S. G.26.B.9.1. Message from 3rd Battery Position G.20 d.5.6. Line of fire laid on enemy's position G.29.d.1.6. Range 1,800. Message from Ammn Column. Position N of HARTS ROUGH at S of point 308. Time occupied 12.30 p.m. ⁂⁂⁂⁂⁂⁂⁂

CONFIDENTIAL

WAR DIARY of

2/1st SOUTH MIDLAND (Glos) BRIGADE, R. F. A.

From 1st February, 1916 to 29th February, 1916

****

Volume No.3.

Army Form C. 2118

WAR DIARY
or
INTELLIGENCE SUMMARY

(Erase heading not required.)

Instructions regarding War Diaries and Intelligence Summaries are contained in F.S. Regs., Part II. and the Staff Manual respectively. Title Pages will be prepared in manuscript.

Place	Date	Hour	Summary of Events and Information	Remarks and references to Appendices
INGATESTONE ESSEX	1916 Feby 1st		Cpl R.H.W.Madiock to be 2/Lieutenant (on probation) 13th January, 1916	
	2nd		C.R.A. Inspected 1st Battery in 15pr Gun Drill.	
			Bde took part in Tactical Exercise under Sir.J.Barnsley, V.D. at village of BROOK STREET on BRENTWOOD - LONDON Road. 23 Officers 295 N.C.O's and men, 12 18pr Guns, 29 Wagons and 278 Horses turned out and took part.	
	3rd		Captain A.G.Noble returns to duty from overseas. Inoculation of men.	
	4th		Major E.J.Dunscombe member of District Court Martial held at Baddow House, GT.BADDOW. 2/Lieut.M.J.Richards attended for instruction. 2/Lieut.G.H.J.Lascelles appointed Member of Formation Quartering Committee.	
	5th		D.D.V.S. Central Force inspected contact Mange cases of Brigade.	
	6th	10a.m	Capt.C.K.S.Metford reported for duty. Church Parade	
	9th		Brigade Major inspected 2nd Battery at 15 pr. Gun Drill. C.R.A. Inspected Ammunition Column.	
	11th		Range party proceeded to SOUTHMINSTER by march route. 15 Men and Horses	
	12th		Depot (3rd) Battery proceeded to SOUTHMINSTER by march route. 5 Officers 130 other ranks 65 Riding and 56 Light Draught Horses. 6 15pr Guns and 4 G.S.Wagons.	
	13th		Dismounted party proceeded to SOUTHMINSTER by train 8.35 a.m. 12 Officers 119 Other Ranks Capt.C.K.S.Metford transferred to 2/1st Divisional Ammunition Column	

1875 Wt. W593/826 1,000,000 4/15 J.B.C. & A. A.D.S.S./Forms/C.2118.

Army Form C. 2118

WAR DIARY
or
INTELLIGENCE SUMMARY

(Erase heading not required.)

Instructions regarding War Diaries and Intelligence Summaries are contained in F. S. Regs., Part II. and the Staff Manual respectively. Title Pages will be prepared in manuscript.

Place	Date	Hour	Summary of Events and Information	Remarks and references to Appendices
INGATESTONE ESSEX	1916 Feby 14th		Firing practice at SOUTHMINSTER	
	15th		Firing practice at SOUTHMINSTER. I.O.M. inspected 18pr Equipment. All Horses inspected by D.A.D.R. No.2 Circle, Eastern Command as to their fitness for Foreign Service.	
	17th		Dismounted party returned from SOUTHMINSTER. All Horses inspected by A.D.V.S. 61st Divn.	
	18th		10 Civilian &. Bain and 3 Old G.S.Wagons on charge of Ammunition Column sent to A.S.C. field CHELMSFORD for disposal.	
	19th		56 Horses sent to North Midland Veterinary Hospital, LUTON. Major E.J.Dunscombe appointed President Quartering Committee, R.A. 61st Divn Vice Lt.Col Cox.	
	20th	10a.m	2/Lieut.M.J.Richards attends 4 weeks Course at SHOEBURYNESS. Church parade.	
	22nd		Inoculation of Officers & men. Court of Enquiry held on "Illegal Absence" of 1868 Sergt.Morgan, E.F. President Capt.G.S.James Members 2/Lt.Friend and 2/Lt.Ryder.	
	24th 24-25th		Depot Battery and Range Party returned from SOUTHMINSTER. Period of Viligence. Indents for Iron & Field Rations ready to hand in, and Bde prepared to move at short notice	
	25th		C.R.A. inspected Gun Pits erected by 1st Battery at MILL GREEN	
	26th		Capt.Wagons, James and G.S. Horses and G.S Horses from 61st Divisional Train joins for duty All unserviceable and civilian wagons returned to A.S.C. CHELMSFORD. Only new Equipment now in possession	

1875 Wt. W 593/826 1,000,000 4/15 J.B.C. & A. A.D.S.S./Forms/C. 2118.

Army Form C. 2118

WAR DIARY
or
INTELLIGENCE SUMMARY

(Erase heading not required.)

Instructions regarding War Diaries and Intelligence Summaries are contained in F. S. Regs., Part II. and the Staff Manual respectively. Title Pages will be prepared in manuscript.

Place	Date	Hour	Summary of Events and Information	Remarks and references to Appendices
INGATESTONE ESSEX	1916— Feb 26th & 27th		Brigade moved to No.7 CAMP, BULFORD, SALISBURY PLAIN.	
BULFORD	29th		2/Lieuts Perowne, Rowden, W.J. Baly and Friend attends Artillery School of Instruction, No.14 Camp, LARKHILL, to observe practice of 41st Divl Artillery. C.R.A visited No.7 CAMP.	
			************	
			(Unless otherwise specified, Drill is carried out daily under Battery arrangements)	

1875 W₁. W503/826 1,000,000 4/15 J.B.C. & A. A.D.S.S./Forms/C. 2118.

Army Form O. 1810
All Arms.

Each issue of orders will be numbered consecutively throughout the year. A fresh series will be commenced with the first issue in each year.

Unit _____

DAILY ORDERS. Part II.

No. _1_

Station
Date _February 5th 1916_

Sub. No. of Order.	Subject.	Regimental No., Rank and Name.			Sqdn. Batty or Co.	Particulars of Casualties &c., and date
		No	Rank			
		2645	Gr.	Mason W. J.	HQ	
		2099	"	Greaves J. H.	1st Bty	Granted Leave from 1-2-16 to 8-2-16
		3030	"	Walters H.		
		946	Cpl.	Rayers A.		
		244	QMS	Saunders G.		
		2281	Gr.	Doughty G.	2nd Bty	
		3028	"	Rivers J.		
		2855	Dr.	Williams R.		
		2619	Gr.	Law W. H.	3rd Bty	
		940	Bdr.	Grubb W.		
		2926	Gr.	Burch C.		
		2539	a/Bdr.	Hall R.	Am Col.	
		2471	Dr.	Griffin J.		
		2831	Gr.	Vaux J.		
		2622	Dr.	Lough G.		
		425	a/SS	Smith A. P.	a/Col	Granted Leave from 4-2-16 to 11-2-16
		2664	Gr.	Morris A.	Am Col	

Officer Commanding or Adjutant.

J. C. Disney
Capt. & Adjt.
For O.C. 2nd South Midland F.A. Brigade.

Army Form O. 1810
All Arms.

Each issue of orders will be numbered consecutively throughout the year. A fresh series will be commenced with the first issue in each year.

Unit _____

DAILY ORDERS. Part II.

No. 2

Station _____
Date February 5th 1916

Sub. No. of Order.	Subject.	Regimental No., Rank and Name		Sqdn. Batty or Co.	Particulars of Casualties &c., and date	
		No	Rank			
		2913	Dr.	Walker W	Am Col	To Hospital 30-1-16
		2350	Gr.	Tyler B		
		2405	Dr.	Cookson J.G.	1st Bty	From Hospital 3-2-16
		2924	"	Partridge R	"	" 29-1-16
		2578	"	Jennings J	"	" 31-1-16
		2052	Gr.	Rea A.E	2nd Bty	" 2-2-16
		2119	Dr.	Edwards J		" 2-2-16
		2018	"	Saunders J		" 3-2-16
		424	Gr.	Hayter W.H.		" 30-1-16
		1000	Dr.	Willis F		" 31-1-16
		2068	Gr.	Field E	3rd Bty	" 1-2-16
		974	"	Grubb T		" 3-2-16
		2194	Sdr.	Daniels S		" 5-2-16
		3055	Gr.	Cinderbury		" "
		2240	Dr.	Chantler W		" "
		2488	Gr.	Gillam J.W.	Am Col	29-1-16
		466	Dr.	Sollars T	A.S.C	" "
			2/Lieut	Turner H.D.	Am Col	Proceeds to Arty School HAVERNAS 30-1-16
		1038	Cpl.	James A.	ditto	ditto 30-1-16
		2908	Gr.	Jones G (servant)		

Officer Commanding or Adjutant.

Army Form O. 1810
All Arms.

Each issue of orders will be numbered consecutively throughout the year. A fresh series will be commenced with the first issue in each year.

Unit _____

DAILY ORDERS. Part II.

No. 5

Station _____
Date February 5 - 1916

Sub. No. of Order.	Subject.	Regimental No., Rank and Name.			Sqdn. Batty or Co.	Particulars of Casualties &c., and date	
		No	Rank				
		3210	Gr.	Ricketts J.D.		Reinforcements	
		3184	"	Spilsbury W.	2nd Bty	joined from Base	2-2-16
		3431	"	Weaver W.			
		3223	"	Page. A. P.			
		3339	"	Barrow R.			
		803	Bdr	Vale. E.	3rd Bty	Completed A.F.W 3126 proceeds on 1 months leave, struck off strength	1-2-16
			2/Lieut	Gadie C.A.	2/2nd West Riding Bde RFA	Attached for 14 days instruction from	1-2-16
		3598	Dr.	Hart. A.	3rd Bty	Reinforcements joined from Base	2-2-16
		3510	"	Taylor. G.			
		3074	Dr.	Hobbs. F.	Am Col	to 29 CCS. 30/1/16 struck off strength	2-2-16
		3043	Gr.	Wainwright S.	ditto	transferred to HQ	4-2-16
			2/Lieut	Lane W.H.	1st Bty	To hospital	4-2-16
		2119	Dr.	Edwards. J.	2nd	" "	30-1-16
		914	"	Hillichip. A.E.		" "	4-1-16
		2194	Bdr	Daniels. G.		" "	31-1-16
		1042	"	Martin. F.		" "	2-2-16
		3055	Gr.	Cinderbury	3rd "	" "	" "
		2240	Dr.	Chantler W.		" "	" "
		2234	"	Styles J.		" "	3-2-16

Officer Commanding or Adjutant.

Army Form O. 1810
All Arms.

Each issue of orders will be numbered consecutively throughout the year. A fresh series will be commenced with the first issue in each year.

Unit
DAILY ORDERS. Part II.

No. 4

Station
Date February 5th 1916

Sub. No. of Order.	Subject.	Regimental No., Rank and Name	Sqdn. Batty or Co.	Particulars of Casualties &c., and date	
		No. Rank		St Omer	
		2/Lieut Allen B.H.B.	1st Bty	To artillery advisor	30-1-16
		" ditto		re'd from ditto	
				(ref permanent com: (Regular Army))	
		Major Lattey J.C.	1st Bty	on course of Senior Arty Offrs	31-1-16
		" ditto		from ditto	5-2-16
	24/61	Gr Saunders W.		on "	31-1-16
		" ditto		from "	5-2-16
		2/Lieut Hall. A.W.	190th Bde RFA	Attached for	
		" Roberts H.J.	189th "	14 days instruction from	1-2-16
	2426	Gr Drew F.G.	1st Bty	attached to 48th Divl H.Q. RA	31-1-16
	3135	Dr Ayris T.J.	ditto	Reinforcement Joined from D.a.C.	2-2-16
	2324	Gr Burgess J.H.	ditto	transferred from Am Col	5-2-16
	332	Bdr Cook L.	2nd	appointed Rough Rider authority. Art: 900. Royal Warrants	29-1-16
	799	Gr Maullin W.	2nd Bty	Completed A.F.W. 3126 proceeded on months leave Struck off strength	1-2-16
	844	" Gwillam A.			
	880	S/Sr Hughes H.			
	2292	Gr Delahey J.	ditto	To No. 4 CCS 3/2/16 struck off strength	4-1-16
	3054	Gr Trayhearn D.A.	H.Bty	appointed Fitter	1-2-16

Officer Commanding or Adjutant.

Army Form O. 1810.
All Arms.

Each issue of orders will be numbered consecutively throughout the year. A fresh series will be commenced with the first issue in each year.

Unit _____

DAILY ORDERS. Part II.

No. 5

Station _____

Date 13th February 1916

Imp. Hav. — 5.009

Sub. No.of Order.	Subject.	Regimental No., Rank and Name.	Sqdn. Batty or Co.	Particulars of Casualties &c., and date	
		No	Rank		
		981	Gr	Potter J.L.	1st Bty	To be paid a/Bdr in place of 2015 a/Bdr Underhill. (Struck off Strength)	from 2/1/16
		2454	Gr	Fisher H.	do	Struck off strength authority 3rd Army. AC/491	4/2/16
		1016	Gr	Evans G.H.	2nd "	Allotment of Pay 6d per day	9/2/16
		932	Gr	Havins J	do	To No 4 CCS struck off strength	8/2/16
			2/Lieut	Woodward G.R.	do	To ENGLAND	9/2/16
		2171	Dr	Jones A.W.	do	To BASE struck off strength	20/1/16
		1030	Gr	Brooks F.	do	Killed in action	11/2/16
		2234	Dr	Stypler J	3rd "	To No 4 CCS struck off strength	10/2/16
		2032	Dr	Foster J.W.	Am Col	To BASE struck off strength	15/1/16
		424	Gr	Hayter W.H.	3rd Bty	Joined from D.a.C	13/11/15
			2/Lieut	Sellars G	Am Col	Joined from 2/2/317B-RFA	10/2/16
			2/Lieut	Liner H.D.	Am Col	Returned from Artillery Course HAVERNAS	11/2/16
		1038	Cpl	James A			
		2908	Gr	Jones G (servant)			

Officer Commanding or Adjutant.

Army Form O. 1810
All Arms.

Each issue of orders will be numbered consecutively throughout the year. A fresh series will be commenced with the first issue in each year

Unit _____

DAILY ORDERS. Part II.

No. 6

Station _____
Date 12th February 1916

Sub. No. of Order.	Subject.	Regimental No., Rank and Name	Sqdn. Batty or Co.	Particulars of Casualties &c., and date	
		No. Rank			
		959 Gr Boddentary J	HQ	To Hospital	10/2/16
		2/Lieut Allen B H S	1st Bty	" "	12/2/16
		2164 Gr Cullen F C W	2nd Bty	" "	5/2/16
		859 " Harrison F J	" "	" "	5/2/16
		932 " Havins J	" "	" "	6/2/16
		2862 Gr Williams W	3rd	" "	12/2/16
		2088 Gr Duffield G	Am Col	" "	8/2/16
		494 Bdr Cox W	1st Bty	From Hospital	8/2/16
		2164 Gr Cullen F C W	2nd	" "	11/2/16
		1042 Bdr Martin G	3rd	" "	11/2/16
		2913 Sd Tyler B	Am Col	" "	8/2/16
		2350 Gr Baker A	" "	" "	8/2/16
		2088 Dr Duffield G	" "	" "	12/2/16

Officer Commanding or Adjutant.

Army Form O. 1810.
All Arms.

Each issue of orders will be numbered consecutively throughout the year. A fresh series will be commenced with the first issue in each year.

Unit _____

DAILY ORDERS. Part II.

No. 4

Station _____

Date 12th February 1916

Sub. No. of Order.	Subject.	Regimental No., Rank and Name	Sqdn. Batty or Co.	Particulars of Casualties &c., and date
		No / Rank		
		Cpl Hearn A.S. (AVC)	HQ	
		2844 Gr Youngjohns H	HQ	
		2051 Bdr Hicklin WH		
		2031 Dr Rouse EW	1st Bty	Granted
		2056 " Penney A.C.		Leave from
		2248 a/Bdr Rogers W		8/2/16 to
		2163 Dr Richards H	2nd Bty	15/2/16
		2964 Gr Oliver L.C.		
		992 a/Bdr Saunders H		
		2960 Dr Horcott J.	3rd Bty	
		1058 Gr Beaman J		
		1039 a/Bdr Pritchard W		
		3031 Gr Williams E	Am Col	
		2294 Dr Lamputt W		
		347 Gr Baskerville P.J.	3rd Bty	Granted Leave from 11/2/16 to 18/2/16

Officer Commanding or Adjutant.

Army Form O. 1810
All Arms.

Each issue of orders will be numbered consecutively throughout the year. A fresh series will be commenced with the first issue in each year.

Unit
DAILY ORDERS. Part II.

No.

Station
Date 17 February 1916

Sub. No. of Order.	Subject	Regimental No., Rank and Name	Sqdn. Batty or Co.	Particulars of Casualties &c., and date	
		2099 Dr Greaves G	1st Bty	Admitted to Hospital with Shrapnel wound in Shoulder	15/2/16
		3046 Dr Hammond E	do	To Hospital	16/2/16
		2341 " Buckley A E	2nd	" "	16/2/16
		2843 " Gunster J	do	" "	16/2/16
		2360 " Bowley W	3rd	" "	15/2/16
		1042 Bdr Martin G	.	" "	15/2/16
		2416 Dr Cole G	Amb	" "	14/2/16
		2493 " Slade H	"	" "	14/2/16
		2/Lieut Lane N W	.	From Hospital	13/2/16
		2088 Dr Duffield G	.	" "	12/2/16
		989 Cr Hoddenham J	HQ	" "	13/2/16
		2622 Dr Louch J	A Bat	Admitted to Birmingham Hospital (while on leave)	4/2/16

Army Form O, 1810
All Arms.

Each issue of orders will be numbered consecutively throughout the year. A fresh series will be commenced with the first issue in each year.

Unit _____

DAILY ORDERS. Part II.

No. 9

Station _____
Date 19th February 1916

Imp. Hav. — 5,000

Sub. No. of Order.	Subject.	Regimental No., Rank and Name.			Sqdn. Batty or Co.	Particulars of Casualties &c., and date
		No	Rank			
		2216	a/Bdr	Manfylde. S	H.Q.	Promoted to Bdr vice 541 – Bdr Harbron W – to Base for discharge 14/1/16 } 15/1/16
		554	Sgt.	Sheldon. W	A. Col.	Promoted to S/Major vice S/M Hayward, to BASE for discharge } from 9/2/16
		991	Cpl	Hickman. E	A. Col.	Promoted to Sgt vice Sheldon } from 9/2/16
		992	Bdr	Perry. J	" "	" Cpl vice Hickman
		2483	a/Bdr	Summers H.E	" "	" Bdr vice Perry
		3434	Gr.	Woodings. J	" "	" a/Bdr vice Summers
		2230	a/Bdr	Willis. A.E	" "	" Cpl vice Cpl Evans evacuated } from 28/12/15
		1029	Gr.	Wise. E	" "	" a/Bdr vice a/Bdr Willis 28/12/15
		2255	Bdr	Canty. H.	3rd Bty	" Cpl vice Cpl Crow evacuated 24/12/15
		2414	a/Bdr	Coombs. J	" "	" Bdr vice Bdr Canty 24/12/15
		2244	Gr.	Whitford H.	" "	" a/Bdr vice a/Bdr Coombs 24/12/15
		803	Bdr	Vale. E.	" "	" Cpl vice Cpl Harris evacuated 30/1/16
		2947	a/Bdr	Jones. A.	" "	" Bdr vice Bdr Vale 30/1/16
		2213	Gr.	Potter. J.	" "	" a/Bdr vice a/Bdr Jones 30/1/16

Officer Commanding or Adjutant.

Army Form O. 1810
All Arms.

Each issue of orders will be numbered consecutively throughout the year. A fresh series will be commenced with the first issue in each year.

Unit _____

DAILY ORDERS. Part II.

No. 10

Station _____
Date 19th February 1916

Sub. No. of Order.	Subject.	Regimental No., Rank and Name.		Sqdn. Batty or Co.	Particulars of Casualties &c., and date
		No	Rank		
		2/Lieut.	Perrins C J R	1st Bty	
		2475 Gr.	Groves W J	HQ	
		1084 Sgt	Rouse A W	1st Bty	
		2113 Cpl.	Brettell G		
		2163 Dr	Richards F		Granted Leave
		966 "	Winter J	2nd Bty	from 15/2/16
		952 "	Beard G		
		2994 a/Bdr	Justin C	3rd Bty	to 22/2/16
		2252 Gr.	Hawkeswood B		
		2287 "	Baylis A		
		2610 "	Lewis W	Am Cok	
		3064 Dr	Barber J		
		854 Gr.	Harrison F J	2nd Bty	To No 19 CCS struck off strength 19/2/16
		308 Sgt	Warby H	3rd Bty	To ENGLAND 29/1/16 Munition Work struck off strength 29/1/16
		2144 Cpl.	Harris S		
		425 Gr	Carpenter J	do	Joined from L of C 13/11/15
		2962 Gr	Hughes W E	HQ	Allotment of Pay 6d per day. Name changed from Emma Evans to Emma Hughes MARRIED 23/11/15 necessary papers forwarded

Officer Commanding or Adjutant.

Army Form O. 1810
All Arms.

Each issue of orders will be numbered consecutively throughout the year. A fresh series will be commenced with the first issue in each year.

Unit _____

DAILY ORDERS. Part II.

No. 11

Station
Date February 19th 1916

Sub. No. of Order.	Subject.	Regimental No., Rank and Name	Sqdn. Batty or Co.	Particulars of Casualties &c., and date	
		No Rank			
		2682 Gr. Price E.J	1st Bty	Appointed Fitter in place of No. 2454 Ftr Fisher H. struck off strength 4/2/16 = To date from	5/2/16
		1019 Dr. Haynes C	do	Awarded 4 days Field Punishment No 2 / = 19/2/16	
		3289 Gr. Evans H.R	do	Joined from Reinforcements	16/2/16
		1091 Gr. Twining F.H.J	do	Granted II Class Proficiency Pay from	5/8/15
		2/Lieut Hall A.W ("A" Bty 190 Bde RFA) 2/Lieut Roberts H.L ("C" Bty 189 Bde RFA)		Returned from Course to ENGLAND	14/2/16
		864 Sgt. Mixon C.G	2nd Bty	Allotment of Pay to wife 1/- per day allotment to Dependant cancelled	24/1/16
		2/Lieut Thacker J. 2692 Gr. Maiden W.H (Servant)	3rd Bty "	Proceed on Arty Course	14/2/16
		2/Lieut Gadie C.H (2/2 West Riding Bde RFA)		Returned from Course to ENGLAND	14/2/16
		3397 Dr. Belcher C	3rd Bty	Joined from Reinforcements	16/2/16

Officer Commanding or Adjutant.

Army Form O. 1810.
All Arms.

Each issue of orders will be numbered consecutively throughout the year. A fresh series will be commenced with the first issue in each year.

Unit _____

DAILY ORDERS. Part II.

No. 12

Station
Date 26th February 1916

Sub. No. of Order.	Subject.	Regimental No., Rank and Name.			Sqdn. Batty or Co.	Particulars of Casualties &c., and date	
		No	Rank				
		528	Dr.	Weavers. A.	2nd Bty	To hospital	18/2/16
		2811	Gr.	Franter F.	" "	" "	22/2/16
		2699	Dr.	Powell. F.	" "	" "	22/2/16
		528	"	Weavers. A.	" "	" "	23/2/16
		997	a/Bdr	Saunders H.	" "	" "	20/2/16
		2482	Gr.	Grazier E.	" "	" "	20/2/16
		3396	Dr.	Baddeley E.A.	" "	" "	23/2/16
			2/Lieut	Allen B.H.B	1st "	From "	20/2/16
		528	Dr.	Weavers. A.	2nd "	" "	21/2/16
		2699	"	Powell. F.	" "	" "	25/2/16
		1042	Bdr	Martin G.	3rd "	" "	20/2/16
		2482	Gr.	Grazier E.	" "	" "	24/2/16
		2493	Dr.	Slade A.	Am Col	" "	25/2/16
		3050	"	Bishton G.L.	" "	" "	25/2/16
			2/Lieut	Thacker. W.J.	3 Bty	returned from Arty Course	26/2/16
		2692	Gr.	Maiden. W.H. (servant)	" "		

Officer Commanding or Adjutant.

For information of the A.G.'s Office at the Base.

Officers and men who have become casuals, been transferred or joined since last report.

Place _____ Date 26th February 1916

No 13

Regtl. Number	Rank	Name	Corps	Nature of casualty, or name of unit from or to which transferred	Date of being struck off or coming on the ration return	Remarks*
	2/Lieut	Clements. W.G.	Hd Qrs			
	2/ "	Williams. A.C.	2nd Battery			
2116	Gr.	Miles. S.A.	} 1st "	} Granted Leave from to	22/2/16 29/2/16	
2122	Sptr	Fleming G.H.				
2352	Dr.	Bayes. W.J.				
1031	"	Powell J.				
1416	Pte	Griffiths W. RAMC attached	2nd "			
2244	A/Bdr	Whitford H.	} 3rd "			
999	Dr.	Ramsey E.				
2881	Sptr	Young H.				
2581	Dr.	Jones. F.	} Am Col.			
2442	Gr.	Read R.				
2545	Dr.	Jones. A.	H Qrs.			
3009	Cp.ᶫ S.S.	Williams F.H.	1st Battery	} Granted Leave from to	25/2/16 3/3/16	
	Lieut Col.	Bullock C.C.	Hd Qrs	} Granted Leave from to	21/2/16 2/3/16	

* State whether absence is of a permanent or temporary nature, adding, in the case of casuals from wounds or disease, any available information for communication to the relatives.

Army Form B. 213.

FIELD RETURN.

No. of Report _____

(To be furnished by all arms, services, and departments (except A.S.C. units) to the A. G.'s Office at the Base in accordance with Field Service Regulations, Part II.)

RETURN showing numbers RATIONED by, and Transport on charge of, _____ at _____ Date _____

Detail	Personnel			Animals.								Guns, carriages, and limbers and transport vehicles								Remarks
	Officers	Other ranks	Natives	Horses			Mules		Camels	Oxen	Guns, carriages and limbers, showing description	Ammunition wagons and limbers	Machine guns	Aircraft, showing description	Horsed		Motor Cars	Tractors	Mechanical			Motor Bicycles	Bicycles
				Riding	Draught	Heavy Draught	Pack	Large	Small								4 Wheeled	2 Wheeled			Lorries, showing description	Trucks, showing description	Trailers		
Effective Strength of Unit																								
Details, by Arms attached to unit as in War Establishment:—																								
Total																								
War Establishment																								
Wanting to complete																								
(Detail of Personnel and Horses below)																								
Surplus																								
*Attached (not to include the details shown above)																								
Civilians:— Employed with the Unit Accompanying the Unit																								
Total Rationed ...																								

* In the case of field ambulances, hospitals or depots, the number of patients are to be included here, the names being shown in A. F. A. 36.

_____ Signature of Commander.

_____ Date of Despatch.

For information of the A.G.'s Office at the Base.

Officers and men who have become casuals, been transferred or joined since last report.

Place _____   Date 26th February 1916

No 14

Regtl. Number	Rank	Name	Corps	Nature of casualty, or name of unit from or to which transferred	Date of being struck off or coming on the ration return	Remarks*
66	BSM	Heath R	3rd Battery	Rejoined from Months leave taken on strength	20/2/16	
929	Cpl	Franklin H	3rd Battery	on Trench Mortar Course	26/1/16	
1041	"	James A	do	Authority III Army No G 124/112 dated 5/1/16 48th Div No 995 AX dated 20/2/16		struck off strength
2951	Gr.	Hales F	do			
425	"	Carpenter J	do			
344	Gr.	Baskerville P.T.	3rd Battery	Joined from Ba 6	13/11/15	
2183	Gr.	Vause J	Am Column	admitted to BIRMINGHAM hospital (while on leave)	8/2/16	
3100	Dr	Morris R	do	Discharged from hospital to BASE	7/1/16	Struck off strength
3100	"	do	do	Joined as reinforcement from BASE	16/2/16	
803	Bdr	Vale E	3rd Battery	on months leave from 1/2/16 to 29/2/16 taken on strength		

* State whether absence is of a permanent or temporary nature, adding, in the case of casuals from wounds or disease, any available information for communication to the relatives.

Army Form B. 213.

FIELD RETURN.

No. of Report _____

(To be furnished by all arms, services and departments (except A.S.C. units) to the A. G.'s Office at the Base in accordance with Field Service Regulations. Part II.)

RETURN showing numbers RATIONED by, and Transport on charge of, _____ at _____ Date _____

DETAIL	Personnel			Animals								Guns, carriages, and limbers, and transport vehicles.									REMARKS
	Officers	Other ranks	Natives	Horses			Mules		Camels	Oxen	Guns, carriages and limbers, showing description	Ammunition wagons and limbers	Machine guns	Aircraft, showing description	Horsed		Motor Cars	Tractors	Mechanical			Motor Bicycles	Bicycles
				Riding	Draught	Heavy Draught	Pack	Large	Small								4 Wheeled	2 Wheeled			Lorries, showing description	Trucks, showing description	Trailers		

Effective Strength of Unit

Details, *by Arms* attached to unit as in War Establishment:—

Total

War Establishment

Wanting to complete
(Detail of Personnel and Horses below)

Surplus

*Attached (not to include the details shown above)

Civilians:—
Employed with the Unit
Accompanying the Unit

TOTAL RATIONED ...

* In the case of field ambulances, hospitals or depots, the number of patients are to be included here, the names being shown in A. F. A. 36.

Signature of Commander.

Date of Despatch.

For information of the A.G.'s Office at the Base.

No 15

Officers and men who have become casuals, been transferred or joined since last report.

Place _____   Date 26th February 1916

Regtl. Number	Rank	Name	Corps	Nature of casualty, or name of unit from or to which transferred	Date of being struck off or coming on the ration return	Remarks*
2426	Gr.	Drew F.G.	1st Battery	Rejoined from Course of instruction in flag signalling	20/2/16	
	Captain	Penney A.V.	do	Gone to ENGLAND on a Course of instruction on ranging etc	21/2/16	
2029	Gr.	Greaves J.H.	do	To C.C.S. and struck off strength	16/2/16	
2284	Gr.	Doughty G.	2nd Battery	Allotment of Pay 6d per day to wife 3/2/16 Dependants allotment cancelled	3/2/16	necessary papers forwarded
54	BSM	Hayward H.	do	Rejoined from Months leave taken on strength	20/2/16	
848	Gr.	Gwilliam A.	do	on months leave from 1/2/16 to 29/2/16		
799	"	Maullin W.	do			
880	Sptr	Hughes H.H.	do	taken on strength		
2928	Dr.	Wiggin A.	3rd Battery	Transferred to ENGLAND per "H.S. "St David"	20/11/15	struck off strength
2425	Gr.	Cooke J.	do	Transferred to ENGLAND per H.S. "St GEORGE"	3/1/16	struck off strength

* State whether absence is of a permanent or temporary nature, adding, in the case of casuals from wounds or disease, any available information for communication to the relatives.

Army Form B. 213.

FIELD RETURN.

No. of Report _____
(To be furnished by all arms, services and departments (except A.S.C. units) to the A. G.'s Office at the Base in accordance with Field Service Regulations. Part II.)

RETURN showing numbers RATIONED by, and Transport on charge of, _____ at _____ Date _____

DETAIL	Personnel			Animals							Guns, carriages, and limbers, and transport vehicles.										REMARKS
	Officers	Other ranks	Natives	Horses			Mules		Camels	Oxen	Guns, carriages and limbers, showing description	Ammunition wagons and limbers	Machine guns	Aircraft, showing description	Horsed		Motor Cars	Tractors	Mechanical			
				Riding	Draught	Heavy Draught	Pack	Large	Small							4 Wheeled	2 Wheeled			Lorries, showing description	Trucks, showing description	Trailers	Motor Bicycles	Bicycles
Effective Strength of Unit																									
Details, by Arms attached to unit as in War Establishment:—																									
Total																									
War Establishment																									
Wanting to complete																									
(Detail of Personnel and Horses below)																									
Surplus																									
*Attached (not to include the details shown above)																									
Civilians:—																									
Employed with the Unit																									
Accompanying the Unit																									
TOTAL RATIONED ...																									

* In the case of field ambulances, hospitals or depots, the number of patients are to be included here, the names being shown in A. F. A. 36.

_____ Signature of Commander.

_____ Date of Despatch.

CONFIDENTIAL

WAR DIARY of

2/1st SOUTH MIDLAND (Glos) BRIGADE, R. F. A.

from 1st March, 1916 to 31st March, 1916

****

Volumn No. 4.

Army Form C. 2118.

WAR DIARY
or
INTELLIGENCE SUMMARY.
(Erase heading not required.)

Instructions regarding War Diaries and Intelligence Summaries are contained in F. S. Regs., Part II. and the Staff Manual respectively. Title pages will be prepared in manuscript.

Place	Date	Hour	Summary of Events and Information	Remarks and references to Appendices
No.7 Camp, BULFORD	1916 March 1st		Advance party proceeded to LARKHILL prior to Batteries moving for firing practice. Range party proceeded for 2 weeks duty on WEST DOWN RANGES. 2/Lieut.Nurse, in charge. Capt.Reid, A.V.C.reported for duty. All horses in Brigade inspected by A.D.V.S. 61st Divn.	
	2nd		Bde Hd Staff and Batteries proceeded to No.22 Canadian Lines, LARKHILL and encamped there during firing practice. 4 Guns 18pr, 4 Firing Battery and 4 G.S. Wagons taken per Battery. Starting Time 9.30 a.m. Order of March H.Q.Staff, 3rd Battery, 2nd Battery, 1st Battery. Supplies sent to LARKHILL daily by Ammunition Column. 9 Baggage Wagons, 9 Drivers and 18 Horses attached during move from INGATESTONE, returned to O/C Hdqr Company, A.S.C. 61st Div. Following Officers left in Camp during firing practice:- 2/Lt. Ryder (i/c Details & Camp) 2/Lt.Friend and 2/Lt.Fenwick.	
LARKHILL	3/7th 4th,6th & 8th		Brigade Firing Practice at WEST DOWN RANGES. During the 3 days of firing,extreme cold weather was experienced. Firing Point Parties supplied by this Brigade to 2/2nd S.M.Bde, RFA on the Ranges	
	3rd		Batteries rendezvous as follows:- H. 1 3 d (TILSHEAD) Training Map. 1st Battery 9.15 a.m. 2nd Battery 11 a.m. 3rd Battery 12 noon. First Battery to rendezvous each day inspected by Major General Brunker, Inspector R.H.& R.F.A.	
BULFORD			24 Remounts arrived from Exeter.	

T.2134. Wt. W708—776. 500000. 4/15. Sir J. C. & S.

Army Form C. 2118.

WAR DIARY
or
INTELLIGENCE SUMMARY.
(Erase heading not required.)

Instructions regarding War Diaries and Intelligence Summaries are contained in F. S. Regs., Part II. and the Staff Manual respectively. Title pages will be prepared in manuscript.

Place	Date	Hour	Summary of Events and Information	Remarks and references to Appendices
LARKHILL	1916 March 5th		Batteries rendezvous NEW BUILDINGS. G.18. d 22. 2nd Battery 9.15 a.m. 3rd Battery 11 a.m. 1st Battery 12 noon.	
BULFORD	6th		Church Parade. Notice given for all lettering on Wagons to be obliterated. Capt.Groves acting Medical Officer to Details left in Camp during the absence at LARKHILL of Lieut.Hutchinson, R.A.M.C. 20 L.D. & 10 Riding Horses arrived from WORCESTER.	
LARKHILL	7th		Batteries rendezvous B.25 d, 9.7. EAST DOWN FARM. 3rd Battery 9.15 a.m. 1st Battery 11 a.m 2nd Battery 12 noon.	
BULFORD	8th		2/Lt.Bryant joined for duty and posted to Ammunition Column. Following remounts arrived:- 54 L.D. from SHIREHAMPTON, 32 L.D. from PETERSFIELD and 34 L.D. from ORMSKIRK.	
	9th		Hd Qr Staff and Batteries returned to No.7 Camp, BULFORD from LARKHILL. Starting Time 10 a.m Order of March:- H.Q.Staff, 1st 2nd 3rd Batteries and Baggage Waggons. Mr.Locke (Engineer G.P.O) attached to this Brigade as Instructor in Telephony.	
	10th		1st Battery took part with 184th Inf Bde in a Tactical Exercise. Scheme to storm QUARLEY HILL (2 miles E of CHOLDERTON) from the West. Battery took up position at WARREN FARM. Blank ammunition used. / All horses inspected by Inspector of Remounts (Col.Ferrers) Medical Board at PERHAM DOWN on men not likely to be fit for overseas	

T2134. Wt. W708—776. 500000. 4/15. Sir J. C. & S.

Army Form C. 2118.

WAR DIARY
or
INTELLIGENCE SUMMARY.
(Erase heading not required.)

Instructions regarding War Diaries and Intelligence Summaries are contained in F. S. Regs., Part II. and the Staff Manual respectively. Title pages will be prepared in manuscript.

Place	Date	Hour	Summary of Events and Information	Remarks and references to Appendices
No.7 Camp, BULFORD	1916 March 11th		Capt.B.Ison joined for duty and posted to Ammunition Column.	
	12th		Church Parade. Mobilization S.A.A. (15 tons) drawn from TIDWORTH.	
	13th		Brigade inspected by G.O.C. on parade. Authority given for the issue of 2 extra lbs of oats for L.D.Horses in Stables. Inspection of Guns by I.O.M. Medical Board at PERHAM DOWN on men not likely to be fit for overseas.	
	14th		12 G.S.Wagons returned by Ammunition Column to Ordnance Officer, TIDWORTH. 1 Wagons Limbered for S.A.A. collected from TIDWORTH.	
	15th		2/Lieut.Roberts detailed to represent Brigade at a Garrison Board on Camp Traffic at office of O/C A.S.C. BULFORD. 9 L.D. Horses arrived from GOSPORT.	
	16th		2nd Battery took part in a Tactical Scheme with 182nd Inf Bde. Inspection of Horses by C.R.A. The following 2/Lieutenants gazetted Temporary Lieutenants:- 2/Lts Fielding,J.C. Rowe, P.T. Dickenson, S.L. and Ostler, E.S.L.	
	17/18th		Gun Epaulments etc dug at night. One Section per Battery dug in S of BULFORD CAMP. Commenced 7 p.m. finished 6 a.m.	
	17th		Following Remounts from:- 16 L.D. from GLOUCESTER, 24 L.D. from SHERBOURNE and 12 L.D. RUGBY.	
	18th		Lieutenant Ostler appointed Brigade Signalling Officer. Captain C.K.S.Metford attached to 2nd Battery from D.A.C. 61st Divn.	

Army Form C. 2118.

WAR DIARY
or
INTELLIGENCE SUMMARY.
(Erase heading not required.)

Instructions regarding War Diaries and Intelligence Summaries are contained in F.S. Regs., Part II. and the Staff Manual respectively. Title pages will be prepared in manuscript.

Place	Date	Hour	Summary of Events and Information	Remarks and references to Appendices
No.7 Camp, BULFORD	1916 March 19th		Church Parade.	
	20th		2/Lieut.Baly attends Course of Telephony & Signalling. 8 R. Horses arrived from MAIDENHEAD. Medical Board for Officers at No.1 Hutments, PERHAM DOWN. 8 Riding Horses arrived from PETERSFIELD. Brigade inspected at Tactical Exercise by G.R.A. Rendezvous BULFORD FIELDS	
	21st	8.45 a.m.	Captains Lindres & James returned to duty from attachment overseas. Captain James transferred from Ammunition Column to 1st Battery. Captain Lindres transferred from 1st to 3rd Battery. 8 Riding Horses arrived from TEMPLECOMBE. Capt Lowe reported for duty and attached to 2nd Battery.	
	23rd		Captain Ison took Command of Ammunition Column. Captain E.S.Harris promoted Temporary Major.	
	24th		Captain Hussey reported for duty and posted to 2nd Battery. 2/Lt.Friend attached to R.A. HdQrs for Staff Duties. 16 Remounts arrived from D.A.Column (ex Gloucester)	
	26th		Church Parade.	
	27th		Lt.Nunn,R.B. reported for duty and posted to 3rd Battery. Captain Hussey transferred from 2nd Battery to 3rd Battery. 2 Riding & 22 L.D. Horses received from BULFORD HOSPITAL. Brigade took part in Divl Artillery Tactical Scheme. Brigade took up positions during early hours of morning.	

Army Form C. 2118.

WAR DIARY
or
INTELLIGENCE SUMMARY.
(Erase heading not required.)

Instructions regarding War Diaries and Intelligence Summaries are contained in F. S. Regs., Part II. and the Staff Manual respectively. Title pages will be prepared in manuscript.

Place	Date	Hour	Summary of Events and Information	Remarks and references to Appendices
No.7 Camp, BULFORD	1916 March 28th		Brigade inspected at Tactical Exercise by C.R.A. Rendezvous ABLINGTON FURZE. Extreme cold weather and blizzard.	
	29th	9 am	Quarterly Audit Board assembled. President Major Hillman.	
	31st		District Court Martial assembled at Officers Mess, 2/1st S.M.Bde, RFA No.7 CAMP, BULFORD for the trial of No.2388 Dr.Griffiths, W. of this Brigade. (This man was sentenced to 28 days detention)	

****

T.J.134. Wt. W708—776. 500000. 4/15. Sir J. C. & S.

61ST DIVISION

305TH BRIGADE R.F.A.

~~MAY - SEP 1916~~

1916 MAY — 1916 SEP

BROKEN UP

Lacks 1-11 Sept 1916   AM 3/10/06
  "   1-4 Aug   "   "   "
  "   1-22 "   "   "   "

305 Bee
R J A

May 1916
late 11 & Dec RJA

May 8p 1

HQ 2nd Div
Vol XXI

2nd DIVISION GENERAL STAFF
No.
Date April 1916

War Diary

General Staff — 2nd Division

April 1916.

Vol 1

CONFIDENTIAL

WAR DIARY

of

305th BRIGADE, RFA
late 2/1 S M Bde
from 22nd May 1916 - to 31st May 1916.

Volume No 1 (Overseas)

WAR DIARY
or
INTELLIGENCE SUMMARY.
(Erase heading not required.)

Army Form C. 2118.

Place	Date	Hour	Summary of Events and Information	Remarks and references to Appendices
AMESBURY. SALISBURY PLAIN.	May 1916 22nd (Monday)	—	Entrained 1/2 Battery at AMESBURY STATION. 1/2 'A' Battery + Bde Hdqrs departed for SOUTHAMPTON at 2.15 p.m. CRATHORPE travelled with second 1/2 'A' Battery). Arrived SOUTHAMPTON 3.55 p.m. Re-embarked "S.S. Herault" at SOUTHAMPTON DOCKS. Left SOUTHAMPTON 6.30pm. Lieut Col 2K/Mitford O/C Boat. 305 Bde only on boat.	Appendix N°1 Train programme. Appendix N°2 'Boat Sta Q.M.M
HAVRE FRANCE	May 23rd (Tuesday)	—	Arrived at port of HAVRE 5 a.m. Calm crossing. Brigade disembarked 9 a.m. marched off to No 5 Docks Rest Camp, about 2 kilos, where remainder of day was spent.	Q.M.M
—	May 24th (Wednesday)	—	Brigade entrained as follows:- Hdqrs & 'A' Bty Point 1 (Gare) Gare de Voyage. 7.30 a.m. 'B' Battery Point 6 Gare de Voyage 8.30 a.m. 'C' Battery Point 3 Gare de Voyage. 12.30 a.m. Bde Hdqrs left HAVRE 9.59 a.m. Route:- MONTEROLIER BUCHY arrived 15.33 departed 16.16. Watered + fed. ABBEVILLE- arrived 21.45 departed 22.25 watered + fed. ST OMER (5.45) HAZEBROUCK (6.30) BERREQUE (ingoing station)	
—	May 25th (Thursday)	—	MERVILLE 7.40 arrived 10 a.m. marched off to HAVERSKERQUE 13.30. 5 Kilos. turned into billets. "B" Bty arrived HAVERSKERQUE 17.30 'C' Bty	Billets Q.M.M Appendix N° 3

Army Form C. 2118.

WAR DIARY
or
INTELLIGENCE SUMMARY.
(Erase heading not required.)

Instructions regarding War Diaries and Intelligence Summaries are contained in F.S. Regs., Part II. and the Staff Manual respectively. Title pages will be prepared in manuscript.

Place	Date	Hour	Summary of Events and Information	Remarks and references to Appendices
HAVERSKERQUE	May 28th 1916 (Sunday)	10:30 8:30	Open Air Service. Horse to Lieut. ST. VENANT – lecture for all Officers by Lt-Gen K.C.B. HARING. R.C.B. Comdg XI Corps. Lt S. Duncan reported on duty & posted to "B" Battery	Order of Battle attended by Lt-Gen...
	May 29th Monday	3pm	Afternoon – "Tear" Batteries from Bergues. Lt-Col Mitford – Major Kearic Capt Howe. Capt Lowe 3/D May proceed by car to No 10 Squad RFC CHOCQUES for 1 hours instruction. On 3 men also from Bde K.1 go for week's instruction on aeroplanes.	AJM
	May 30th Tuesday		Lt-Col Mitford Officially from Indian, 1 Officer per Battery (Majs reserved) from (operational) H Subsection from Bde 16 Apr to 6 Augt. Lt & Toups to D Bn. Battery proceed to LOCON to attached camp to 29th DIV ART on march	
		5pm	Capt Howe, Lt Finbury Brown, Mantel proceed to R.F.C 10 Squad RFC for more hours instruction.	AJM
	May 31st	5pm	Lt Barrow, 3/Lt Maaood McElquhan proceeded to No 10 Squad.	AJM
		4:15pm	RFC to 1 hours instruction. Capt Wolfe represented Bde at conference of Maj Gen trouser RA on 61 DIV ART, 14/25	AJM

Signed M Watts Capt
for OC Comdg 305 Bde RFA

Appendix No. 1

SECRET.

Train No.	Unit.	Officers	Other Ranks	Officers (Horses)	Riding (Horses)	Guns	4-wh.Vehs.	2-wh.Vehs.	Bicycles	Baggage & Stores (tons)	From	To	Starting Day	Starting Time	Arrival Day	Arrival Time
X.1418	2/1 S.M.Cas.Clrg.Stn.	11	82							22	Ludgershall	Southampton Docks.	May 22nd	6.10 am	May 22nd	7.40 am
X.1419	2/7 Rl. Warwick	15	498		32		9	2			"	"	"	7.5 am.	"	8.40 am
X.1420	"	15	497		32		8	2			"	"	"	8.15 am.	"	9.45 am
X.1421	2/8 Rl. Warwick	15	498		32		9	2			"	"	"	9.30 am.	"	11.0 am
X.1422	"B" By. 2/4 S.M.Bde.R.F.A.	2	69		67	2	6	2			Amesbury	"	"	10.20 am.	"	12.5 pm
X.1423	2/8 Rl. Warwick.	15	497		32		8	1			Ludgershall	"	"	11.0 am.	"	12.30 pm
X.1424	"B" By.2/4 S.M.Bde.R.F.A.	2	68		64	2	5	2			Amesbury	"	"	11.15 am.	"	1.0 pm
X.1425	H.Q. 182nd Inf. Bde. (Sec.Div.Sig.Co. Coy. Divl.Train.	7 1 4	27 26 58		25 8 29		6 1 5	1			} Ludgershall	"	"	11.55 am.	"	1.25 pm
X.1426	½"C" By.2/4 S.M.Bde.R.F.A.	2	69		67	2	6	1			Amesbury	"	"	12.10 pm.	"	1.55 pm
X.1427	2/1 S.M.Field.Amb.	10	218		56		14	4			Tidworth	"	"	12.50 pm	"	2.25 pm
X.1428	½"C" By. 2/4 S.M.Bde.R.F.A.	2	68		64	2	5	1			Amesbury	"	"	1.15 pm.	"	3.0 pm.
X.1429	3/1 S.M.Fld.Co. R.E.	3	113		40		6	4	16		Tidworth	"	"	2.0 pm.	"	3.40 pm
X.1430	Bde. Hqtrs. & ½ "A" By. 2/4 S.M.Bde.R.F.A. }	6	111		104	2	7	3			Amesbury	"	"	2.15 pm.	"	3.55 pm
X.1431	½ 3/1 S.M.Fld.Co. R.E.	3	113		41		5	5	5		Tidworth	"	"	3.0 pm.	"	4.40 pm
X.1432	H.Q. Div. R.A. ½"A" By. 2/4 S.M.Bde.R.F.A. }	3 2	20 68	6	14 64	2	2 5	1	17		} Amesbury	"	"	3.30 pm.	"	5.10 pm
X.1435	Divisional Hdqrs.	18	93	6	73		5	1			Tidworth	"	"	4.0 pm.	"	5.40 pm

Indicates train sets

BRIGADE STATE   Appendix No 2.

UNIT   —   306 Bde RFA
OFFICERS   —   18 + 1MO + 1 VO + 1 Chaplain att
OTHER RANKS —   442 (Inclusive
                  (5 AVC, 3 RAMC (1 OC) + 10 ASC att

HORSES { O C — 11
        { R   — 145
        { HD   — (10 ASC att)
        { LD   — 257

MULES   —   Nil
PACK   { HORSES   —   Nil
ANIMALS { MULES   —   Nil
GUNS   —   12 - 18pr QF Mk II
G.S. WAGONS   —   Nil (10 ASC attd)
G.S. LIMBERED WAGONS — Nil
OTHER VEHICLES   =   24 - 18pr LIMBERED
                                 AMM'N WAGONS
                        1 LIMBERED TELE-
                          PHONE CART
                        4 COOKS CARTS (2 wh)
                        1 MALTESE
                        3 WATER CARTS
BICYCLES   4.

                        sgd J K Smithford
                             Lt Col
                             Cmdg
27/5/16   306 Bde RFA

Billets of 305th Brigade R.F.A.

		off	men		
1	Provot Delancey	2	40	6 b^y	
2	Hugues Victor	5	95	c b^y	
3	Rollin Flageolet	2	135	6 b^y	
4	Delancey Paul	1		veterinary	
5	Calonne	40 men		H.Q c b^y	
6	Duballe	20 men		c b^y	
7	Dehaine	5	135	a bat^y	
8	Doulet	1 off.	interpreter		
9	Brasserie Vandelle	5 off.	5 hommes	H.Q.	

E. Destangue

ORDER OF BATTLE.   Not to be taken
                                    into the Trenches

61st (SOUTH MIDLAND) DIVISION.

182nd Inf. Bde.	183rd Inf. Bde.	184th Inf. Bde.
Headquarters.	Headquarters.	Headquarters.
2/5th Bn. R.Warwick Regt.	2/4th Bn. Gloucester Regt.	2/4th Bn. Oxford & Bucks L.I.
2/6th Bn. R.Warwick Regt.	2/6th Bn. Gloucester Regt.	2/4th Bn. Royal Berks. Regt.
2/7th Bn. R.Warwick Regt.	2/7th Bn. Worcester Regt.	2/5th Bn. Gloucester Regt.
2/8th Bn. R.Warwick Regt.	2/8th Bn. Worcester Regt.	2/1st Bucks Bn. Ox.& B.L.I.
182nd Bde. Machine Gun Co.[x]	183rd Bde Machine Gun Co.[x]	184th Bde Machine Gun Co.[x]

DIVISIONAL TROOPS.

Divisional Headquarters.

Divisional Mtd. Troops.

C Squadron 1/1 Hants Yeo.
61st (S.M.) Div. Cyclist Co.

61st (S.M.) Divisional Artillery.

305th (S.M.) Brigade R.F.A. (A, B & C. 18pr. Batt^s.)
306th (S.M.) Brigade R.F.A. (A, B & C. 18pr., D How., Batt^s.)
307th (S.M.) Brigade R.F.A. (A, B & C. 18pr., D How., Batt^s.)
308th (S.M.) Brigade R.F.A. (A, B & C. 18pr., D How., Batt^s.)
61st (S.M.) Div. Amm. Col.

61st (S.M.) Divisional Engineers.

61st (S.M.) Div. Signal Coy.
3/1st S.M. Field Coy.
2/2nd S.M. Field Coy.
1/3rd S.M. Field Coy.

Pioneer Bn., 1/5th Bn. Duke of Cornwalls L.I.

61st (S.M.) Divisional Train.

Medical Units.

2/1st S.M. Field Amb.
2/2nd S.M. Field Amb.
2/3rd S.M. Field Amb.

61st (S.M.) Mobile Veterinary Section.

[x] Not yet formed.

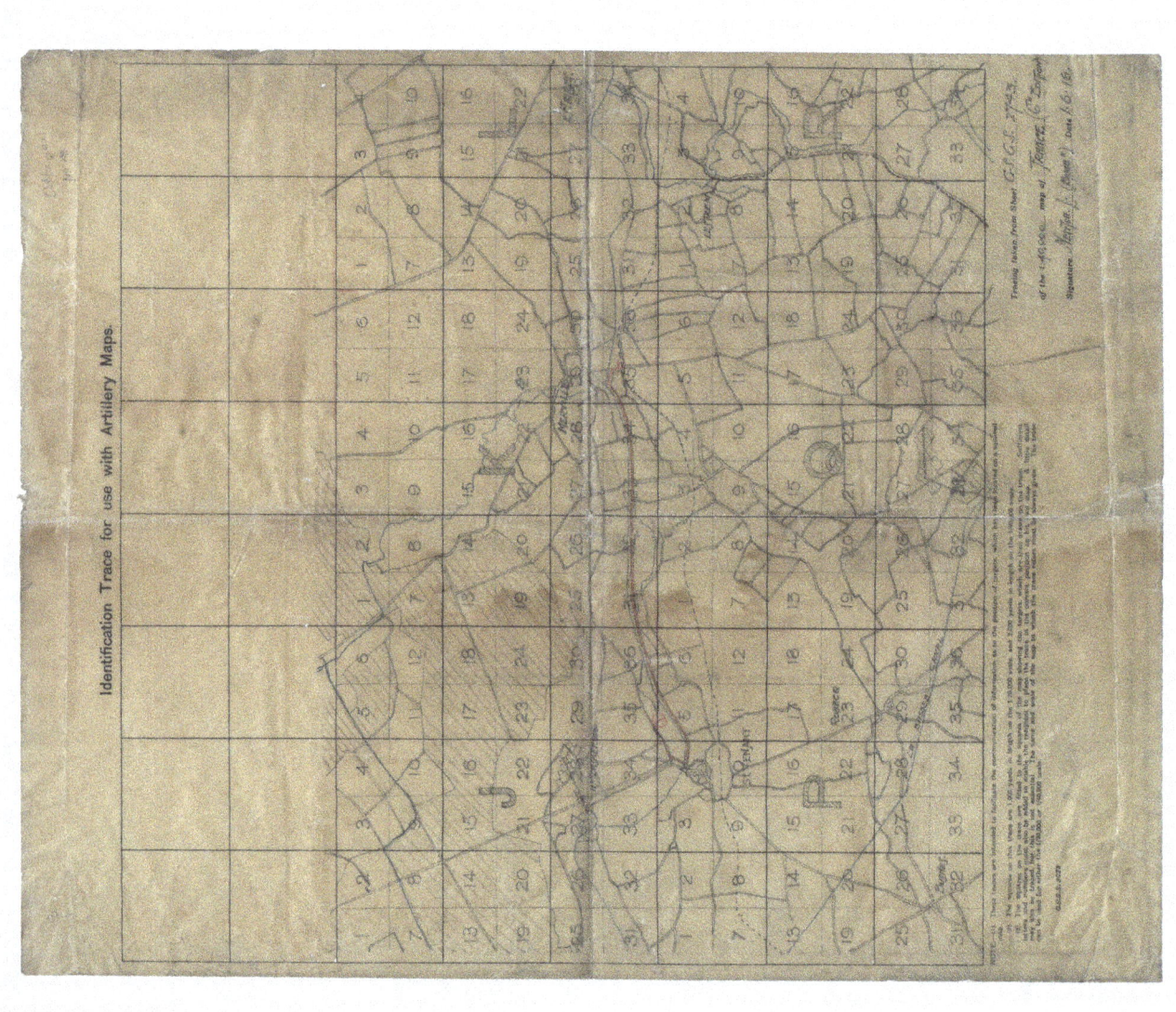

CONFIDENTIAL

War Diary
of
No. 5th Brigade R.F.A.

Army Form C. 2118.

WAR DIARY
or
INTELLIGENCE SUMMARY.
(Erase heading not required.)

Instructions regarding War Diaries and Intelligence Summaries are contained in F.S. Regs., Part II. and the Staff Manual respectively. Title pages will be prepared in manuscript.

Place	Date	Hour	Summary of Events and Information	Remarks and references to Appendices
HAVERSKERQUE	June 1	5.30p	2/Lt A E Bishop attached N° 10 Squad RFC for 1 hours instruction.	a/p
	2		1 man non each Battery attached to N° 18 Anti-Aircraft Section.	a/p
	3		1 Artificer from each Battery attached to 30.M N° 21 Workshops LESTREM.	a/p
			Lt Col J K Stafford & 2/Lt J Daly returned from attachment to 39th Div Art.	a/p
	4	11.10am	Open fire Service.	a/p
	6		4 men from HQ Staff, & 1 Officer 6 Layers & 6 Telephonists per Battery returned from attachment to 39th Div Art.	
			The following proceeded to LOCON for attachment to 39th Div Art:—	
			HQS 2 Officers 4 Other Ranks, 'A' Battery 4 Offrs 35 O.R, 'B' Battery	a/p
			4 Offrs 55 O.R. & 'C' Battery 4 Offrs 46 O.R.	a/p
	8		1 HQ S. Officer returned from attachment to 39 Div Art.	a/p
	10		1 ditto	
			1 N.C.O per Battery proceeded on course of instruction in concreting Gun Emplacements with 33 Div Art.	
	11	10am	Open Air Service.	
			All Officers, N.C.O's & men returned from attachment to 33 Div Art.	a/p

T2134. Wt. W708—776. 500000. 4/15. Sir J. C. & S.

Army Form C. 2118.

WAR DIARY
or
INTELLIGENCE SUMMARY.
(Erase heading not required.)

Instructions regarding War Diaries and Intelligence Summaries are contained in F. S. Regs., Part II. and the Staff Manual respectively. Title pages will be prepared in manuscript.

Place	Date	Hour	Summary of Events and Information	Remarks and references to Appendices
	1916			
	Jun 12		"A" 1/2 "B" & "C" Batteries moved up to firing line to take up positions at :-	
			Firing line Wagon lines.	
			"A" M 16 a 2 6 R 5 c 9 9	
			"B" M 12 a 1 8 R 16 a 8 9	
			"C" M 21 c 7 8 R 11 b 2 2	
			and to form part of Right Group commanded by Lt Col Willock (306 Bde). The Division taking over the Left Sector.	
	" 13		Bde Hdqrs to MERVILLE (as CO is not Commanding Group - not) K 29 & 16.	A/Y/4
			Remaining 1/2 "B" Battery moved up.	A/Y/4
	" 14		Orders received to make up dumps of ammunition at Gun Positions	B/Y/4
			to 500 rounds per Gun 50% H.E. 50% Shrapnel.	
	" 18		Night 17/18" 1/2 "B" Bty moved to unloading position at M 34 c 43 PONT LOGY.	C/Y/4
	" 19		Lt Col S.K. Watford RFA took over command of Bde from Lt Col S.K. Metje a	D/Y/4
	" 20		& also Right Group from Lt Col Willock.	
			Lt Col S.K. Watford returned to England.	E/Y/4

WAR DIARY
or
INTELLIGENCE SUMMARY.
(Erase heading not required.)

Army Form C. 2118.

Place	Date	Hour	Summary of Events and Information	Remarks and references to Appendices
	1916			
	Jan 21	-	HQS moved forward to command group with 6dgrs at LAVENTIE. Following Batteries in group:- A/305 B/305 C/305 A/306 B/306 C/306 D/306(H) C/307 1/2 B/307 (H)	A/M
	24		British Offensive commenced. Daily & nightly Drill programmes of firing for Art.	A/M
	27/28		Night of 27/28. Took part in supporting Infantry bomb attack - after cutting wire on leading down.	A/M
	28/29		Night 28/29 Counter Battery work, supporting left group Infantry bomb attack	A/M
	29/30		Night 29/30 Counter Battery work, supporting attack of 39 Bve on right	A/M

Alfred Noble Capt
Adjutant for
Lt Colonel RFA
Commanding
305th RFA

CONFIDENTIAL

WAR DIARY

305th Bde. R.F.A.

VOLUME 3

July 1st — July 31st
1916

CONFIDENTIAL

War Diary

of

305th Brigade R.F.A.

(Volume No 3 Overseas)

From 1st July 1916   To 31 July 1916

A J Wolfe
Adjutant for OC
305 Bde FA (TF)

Army Form C. 2118.

WAR DIARY
or
INTELLIGENCE SUMMARY.
(Erase heading not required.)

Instructions regarding War Diaries and Intelligence Summaries are contained in F. S. Regs., Part II. and the Staff Manual respectively. Title pages will be prepared in manuscript.

Place	Date	Hour	Summary of Events and Information	Remarks and references to Appendices
	1916 July		2/Lt L Godwin & 2/Lt RM Montgomery joined for duty from B'non. 2/Lt Hargreaves posted to C/305 & 2/Lt Godwin to B/305.	
			Gotha Railway for very deliberate on our front. Tried in vain to bolster. Things settled down all day.	ayu
		4pm	Roads round Armentières shelled. Unfruitful wind would upon answer Fair bursts at Louvetre. A smoke screen. Our turn was worked away towards Linselles. Enemy barrage learner.	ayu ayu ayu ayu ayu ayu
	4		We got it although very insignificant. Our return worth. 5 rounds 4/305. 12 rounds 4/305.	
	6		10 rounds on F/A.5.	
	8		2/Lt Clinnan posted to duty from sick post on 4th.	
	9		Our wire near whiz bang and howitzer shelled.	
			2/Lt S R Callaway & 2/Lt S R Killiam of B/305 ordered Abney head to divisional reserve. Where on night of 11 July nil.	
	11		Got the heavier into action.	
	15		Boches shelled a little to the left. Osl. Know. In a normal way at	ayu

WAR DIARY
or
INTELLIGENCE SUMMARY.
(Erase heading not required.)

Army Form C. 2118.

Place	Date	Hour	Summary of Events and Information	Remarks and references to Appendices
	1916 June		Cmte Group RA taken over by Group of 31 Div Art.	A/H
	16	8.30	Gas attack launched by our troops. Retaliation by enemy	A/H
			Assumed command of new Right Group 6br Div Art, composed of A/305 position at M10.c.8.0. B/305 M10.d.91 A/308 M15 & 84 B/308 M11.c.45 B/30 & M10.c.57. Artillery reinforced by 3 Wire cutting Batteries & How Battery	A/H
			4.7 Mortars etc. from 5th Division. I Motor also attached to special programme of attack.	A/H
			Wadi Battery out wire during morning & wire attacked on heavily causing many casualties	A/H
	17		Attack postponed owing to weather being dull & hazy. Our Artillery fire on 3 Parks Pontoons	A/H
	18		Major G.P. LINDREA B/305 killed in a dug out at OP, a shell carrying the dug out to roof in. He was buried (Roman Catholic) at LALENTE cemetery 19/7/16.	A/H
			Lt T.M DUNCAN assumed command of B/305.	A/H
	19		Bombarded enemy wire FKX outpost. Australian Inf coin (6td) by advanced to attack at up our front RT Battalion (3/h N SPRICH)	A/H

WAR DIARY
or
INTELLIGENCE SUMMARY.
(Erase heading not required.)

Army Form C. 2118.

Instructions regarding War Diaries and Intelligence Summaries are contained in F. S. Regs., Part II. and the Staff Manual respectively. Title pages will be prepared in manuscript.

Place	Date	Hour	Summary of Events and Information	Remarks and references to Appendices
	1916			
	Jan/19		Received orders continuing the enemies trenches but owing to the RIETUN not having succeeded & owing to adverse weather they were withdrawn from advanced positions. HIGH SALIENT bombed very heavily. We expended 29 rounds on our front.	
		1.30	We bombarded H.how 9 - 11 pm & then quietened down	
		21	Quiet day	
		22	Bombarded A105 from OP M6 & A7.9/100 at M.24.d.9.1. 35.E.19 & 86. 31.c 11.6.d.8.5. 8/19. 18.9.26. (No. 4 grs 2 rds of HE) Shot M.21 d.5.2	
		27	Germans bombarded our trenches opposite M.7.b.1.3 & M.N.F. from SNIPER & attempted to raid trenches owing to "A" Co F.F. Pistol. The attempt failed & much heavy loss was inflicted upon the enemy gunners as 9/105 rounds Go through's BIRKF's account was (Artillery record made up by XI Corps Commander.)	
	31	-	Quiet day	

Vol 4

CONFIDENTIAL

WAR DIARY

305. Art Bde

Aug 1st to 31st 1916

VOLUME - 4.

CONFIDENTIAL

War Diary

of

305th Brigade R.F.A.

From 1st August 1916 to 31st August 1916

(Volume 16H Overseas)

WAR DIARY
or
INTELLIGENCE SUMMARY.
(Erase heading not required.)

Army Form C. 2118.

Place	Date	Hour	Summary of Events and Information	Remarks and references to Appendices
In the Field	1916 Aug 4		A Battery at T2 b 4 4 was heavily strafed by our Heavy Battery. Ammunition Dumps blown up.	AWM
	7	3.35am	Enemy blew up large mine at M 30 c 1/2 4. 60 ft deep 160 yds across. Attempted to attack but was repulsed.	AWM
	11		2/Lt E W N May R/Jos transferred to T. M. Battery	AWM
	12	9.15pm	Crater lip of Crater at M 30 c 1/4 4 blown away by us for defensive purposes	AWM
	13		During morning a hostile Battery fired 150 5.9" H E on 136 By R.G.A. at M 5 d 74. 10th Squad R.F.C. were advised and Battery located.	AWM
	14	4.3pm	Small Camouflet mine sprung by us at M 30 a 5 6.	
		8pm	Reported that Germans had broken into one of our Galleries about M 30 c. He was as much surprised as we.	AWM
	15	5 pm	We blew a small mine on Eastern lip of BIRDCAGE Crater blown by enemy at M 30 c 14. Evidence of a 9 cm Bty (old pattern Gun) on this front.	AWM
	16		Enemy blew small mine at M 30 c 4 0. A 77 m/m Battery located at T 1 c 9 1.	AWM

WAR DIARY
or
INTELLIGENCE SUMMARY.

(Erase heading not required.)

Army Form C. 2118.

Instructions regarding War Diaries and Intelligence Summaries are contained in F. S. Regs., Part II. and the Staff Manual respectively. Title pages will be prepared in manuscript.

Place	Date	Hour	Summary of Events and Information	Remarks and references to Appendices
In the field	1916 Aug 17		During morning 2 H.E. howr. Battery fired on our 18pr. Bty. position at M2.c. (3.05) with 120 rds H.E. Position evacuated - no casualties - new position commenced close by. Hostile Battery was located by Kite Balloon near T.9a.4.3.	A/W/R
	18		We became CENTRE GROUP as the Group on our Right (31st Bde) is in Tactical purposes made the RIGHT GROUP under C.R.A. 6th Bde. Some Batteries in our Group i.e. A.R.C/305. A.B/306. B/307. C/169. B/110.	A/W/R
	20	4.40p	Large explosion was seen to take place in direction of BIRTLEY in enemy lines N.19.c.60.	A/W/R
	22	3.45am	10 e blows in our defensive mine at M.30 a 5/7 6.	A/W/R
	23	10.30pm	One of our aeroplanes brought down in Hostile lines.	A/W/R
	24		We raided with small party enemy lines at M.30 a preceded by hurricane torpedo blown at 1.14 am 25th at which time our Batteries fired barrage round point of entry. Raiding party entered killing 3 Germans & meeting with little opposition. Enemy artillery retaliated heavily but caused few casualties to us.	A/W/R

WAR DIARY
or
INTELLIGENCE SUMMARY.
(Erase heading not required.)

Army Form C. 2118.

Place	Date	Hour	Summary of Events and Information	Remarks and references to Appendices
In the Field	1916 Aug		No 2210 Gr F.H. LAWRENCE & No 2047 Gr H.T. JENKINS HQ/305 Bde RFA awarded military medal for gallantry on Jun 19th 1916.	
	24		We again became RIGHT GROUP.	
	26th		Our MOATED GRANGE & CHATEAU REDOUBT OPs used more than normally.	
	28th		During afternoon we paid particular attention to his suspected Trench mortar emplacements firing upon them heavily with 18pr & 5"Hour. Being attacked - we cut wire & bombarded enemys lines with MT Mr.	
		4.45 pm	Gired barrage about BIRDCAGE.	
		4.50 4.51/4.53	Dropped & field gun fire with 3 18pr Batteries.	
		4.53	Gas fire.	
	29		1st Section B/305 attached to C/305 Rt Sec B/305 attached to A/305 for tactical purposes only in their present positions.	
	30		B/170 reformed into a 6 gun Battery, absorbing 2 guns from C/169	
	31		N.V.	

Alfred G.
Capt
Adjutant for the
305 Bde RFA

Vol 5

CONFIDENTIAL

WAR DIARY

Late 305th ART BDE

Sept 1st – 17th. 1916

VOL. V.

CONFIDENTIAL

War Diary

of

305 Brigade R.F.A.

from 1st September 1916 to 17th September 1916.

(Volume No 5 Overseas) Final

Army Form C. 2118.

WAR DIARY
or
INTELLIGENCE SUMMARY.
(Erase heading not required.)

Instructions regarding War Diaries and Intelligence Summaries are contained in F. S. Regs., Part II. and the Staff Manual respectively. Title pages will be prepared in manuscript.

Place	Date	Hour	Summary of Events and Information	Remarks and references to Appendices
L'ARENTIE	Oct 12		HQ of 305 Brigade relieved of command of Right Group b/o Bu Hrs, which was taken over by 306 Bde HQs RFA. (Lt Col Willock)	A/yr A/yr
NOUREAU MONDE		2nd noon	305 Brigade therewith went into rest billets.	
	13th		305 Brigade broken up and absorbed into the Brigades of the 61st Divisional Artillery, making 6 gun Batteries. Lt Col Rowel & Capt Majr A G Mabe with several NCOs men of HQ 5/305 absorbed into HQ S/307. ½ of F/305 to C/307 & ½ to A/306. ½ of A/305 to C/306 & ½ to B/306. ½ of C/305 to F/307 & ½ to B/307. Major E S Harris takes over command of E/306 & Capt T M Dunscon C/306. Brigade closes.	A/yr

A/yr
Capt H arr for
o/c 305 Bde RFA

www.ingramcontent.com/pod-product-compliance
Lightning Source LLC
Chambersburg PA
CBHW081426160426
43193CB00013B/2202